With best

from

FIFTY YEARS OF
BRITISH PARLIAMENT

VOLUME ONE

THE RIGHT HON. H. H. ASQUITH

Prime Minister
Now the Earl of Oxford and Asquith, K. G.

FIFTY YEARS OF
BRITISH PARLIAMENT

BY

THE EARL OF OXFORD AND ASQUITH, K.G.

WITH ILLUSTRATIONS

VOLUME ONE

TORONTO · 1926
S. B. GUNDY · PUBLISHER

PREFACE

THIS book deals with events and matters which are within the range of my own memory. For the best part of the first twenty of the years which it covers, I was an outside spectator; during the remainder I sat in the House of Commons, and ultimately became its Leader. The book does not profess to be, and from the nature of the case it could not be, a detached and impartial survey. It is intended to be a contribution to history written to a large extent from first-hand knowledge. The time with which it is concerned was one of almost ceaseless and often embittered controversies, both between policies and persons, in many of which I took an active part. The imputation, and perhaps the reality, of colour and bias is almost inevitable in a narrative so composed; and without pretending that I have attempted the thankless task of " holding the scales even ", which denudes history of its interest, I have not consciously tampered with the balance.

There is one and, I think, only one relevant topic of capital importance which I have deliberately omitted; the causes of, and our preparations for, the Great War. My reason is twofold: first, that I have already gone over the ground in my book, " The Genesis of the War "; and, next, that since its publi-

cation, there has appeared a more complete and detailed survey in the monumental work, " Twenty-five
Years: 1892–1916 ", by Lord Grey of Fallodon.

I have to acknowledge gratefully the help which
has again been accorded me by Mr. Alexander
Mackintosh, whose wide and accurate knowledge of
our political history, coupled with a rare capacity for
research, has been throughout my work of invaluable
service.

CONTENTS

Part One

viii CONTENTS

ILLUSTRATIONS

PART ONE

CHAPTER I

THE year 1868 is not an inappropriate starting point for a survey of the era in which we live. The death of Lord Palmerston in the autumn of 1865 is sometimes spoken of as marking the opening of a new political and Parliamentary epoch. But in fact the next three years were a time of transition.

It does not fall within the scope of this book to describe Lord Palmerston's career, or to estimate his character. He had sat in sixteen Parliaments, and been a member of every Government except four from 1807 to 1865. The history of his last fifteen years is largely taken up, on its personal side, with a series of rather unedifying manœuvrings between himself and Lord John Russell, as to which of them should be at the top of the Liberal Party. It is curious that so shrewd, and on the whole so dispassionate, an observer as Disraeli should have passed this judgment on him ten years before his death:

" He is really an imposter, utterly exhausted, and at the best only ginger beer and not champagne; and now an old painted pantaloon, very deaf, very blind; here is a man whom the country resolves to associate with energy, wisdom and eloquence, and will until he

has tried and failed."[1] This battered and contempt-
ible figure, after these words were written, was twice
Prime Minister, and died in that office at the age of
eighty, without any trace of physical or mental
failure, the most popular man in England, and having
just received at a general election an emphatic vote
of confidence from the country.

Quite the most remarkable incident in that election
was the rejection of Mr. Gladstone by the University
of Oxford, which enabled him to declare, when he
presented himself as a Liberal candidate to the electors of South Lancashire: "I am come among you
unmuzzled." The new House of Commons, with an
ostensibly Liberal majority, was a Palmerstonian
relic, and is one of the curiosities in our Parliamentary history. In 1866 it refused to pass a milk and
water Reform Bill introduced by the Liberal Government of Lord Russell. In 1867, as the result of an
almost unexampled series of cynical expedients on
the part of Lord Derby and Mr. Disraeli, it established household suffrage in the towns, and added
about a million voters to the electorate which had
been under one million and a half. In 1868 it supported Mr. Gladstone with a reunited Liberal majority, in the first stage of his campaign for Irish
disestablishment, which, only three years before, he
had described as a question that was "remote and
apparently out of all bearing on the practical politics
of the day."[2]

[1] "Letter to Lady Londonderry", Feb. 2, 1855; Buckle, "Life of
Disraeli", III, 567.
[2] Morley, "Life of Gladstone", II, 239.

During the session of 1867, a large and powerful section on both sides of the House of Commons was in open mutiny against their respective chiefs. Mr. Gladstone, whose leadership of the Liberals only dated from the preceding year, more than once contemplated retiring to the independence of the back benches. The famous article in the *Quarterly Review* of that autumn, " The Conservative Surrender ", from the pen of the then Lord Cranborne (afterwards Lord Salisbury), who had already in the House of Commons taunted his party with borrowing their ethics from a political adventurer, shows the contempt, and worse than contempt, in which the writer and his friends in the Tory ranks held Mr. Gladstone's illustrious rival. As late as 1872, Brand, an old and experienced Whip, who had just completed his first session in the Speaker's Chair, records his opinion that " of the two leading men in the House, Gladstone and Disraeli, neither has a strong hold on his followers." [3] They were, in their different ways, two of the greatest Parliamentarians in our history; but when they became, as each did in turn, the idol of the nation, it was not by reason of their ascendancy in the House of Commons, but through their capacity to touch and to capture, the one the imagination, the other the conscience, of their countrymen outside.

[3] Morley, " Gladstone ", II, 390.

CHAPTER II

Clarendon: Ripon

I T is a saying of Burke's that " great men are the
guide posts and landmarks in the State." By the
end of 1868 the leading actors, who had dominated
the political stage during the first half of Queen Victoria's reign, had all bidden it farewell. Of the four
Prime Ministers, who had presided over Governments in the preceding twenty years, Lord Aberdeen
and Lord Palmerston had been removed by death;
Lord Derby, in February, 1868, had retired to make
way for Mr. Disraeli, who had at last, in his own
phrase, " climbed to the top of the greasy pole." The
doyen of them all, Lord Russell, though he lived on
till 1878, had communicated at Christmas in 1867
to Mr. Gladstone and Lord Granville his decision
" on a deliberate view of my past labours, my present
age, and the future anxieties of the State " never to
take office again. The scene was clear for Gladstone
and Disraeli, and for the next decade, and more, they
occupied its forefront.

In the autumn of 1868 a fresh general election
had become inevitable. It was the first held under

LORD CLARENDON

the new franchise, and the last under the old system of hustings nominations, and open voting.[1] The result of the polling was a Liberal majority of 112, though Mr. Gladstone himself, rejected in Lancashire, had to take refuge at Greenwich. " He is much more likely," predicted Charles Dilke, a young Radical just returned for the first time for the new borough of Chelsea, " to become a democratic leader, now that he sits for a big town."

Other newcomers, who were destined to a distinguished Parliamentary future, were, on the Liberal side, Harcourt and Campbell-Bannerman, and on the Conservative side, W. H. Smith, George Hamilton and Henry Chaplin.

Mr. Disraeli resigned without meeting the new Parliament, and Mr. Gladstone formed the first, and what he always considered the best, of the four Cabinets in which he held the office of Prime Minister.[2] There were two or three distinguished members of it (now but dimly remembered) of whom, and of their relations to their chief, it may be convenient at this stage to say something: Lord Clarendon, the Foreign Secretary; Lord Ripon, President of the Council; Mr. Lowe, the Chancellor of the Exchequer; and Mr. Cardwell, Secretary of State for War.

[1] I remember myself, as a schoolboy, standing with a row of others in the open polling booth, and shouting thanks to each elector, who came and recorded his vote for the Liberal candidate.

[2] Curiously enough it turned out to be weak in debating power in the House of Commons. In April, 1870, Phillimore records: " Gladstone feels keenly the want of support in debate. Bright ill; Lowe no moral weight. 'I feel when I have spoken that I have not a shot in my locker.'" Morley, " Gladstone ", II, 296.

Lord Clarendon, though born in a Tory family, may be described as the last of the Whigs. Neither Lord Kimberley (then Lord Wodehouse and Lord Lieutenant of Ireland) nor Lord Ripon was ever a Whig in the pure sense of the term. Kimberley (like Clarendon) came of a Tory stock, and worked his way in complete intellectual independence at Oxford, where he had a distinguished career, to a form of Radicalism, which was unsentimental and in essence utilitarian.

Ripon was born in Downing Street, in one of the few months during which his father, Lord Goderich, the "transient and embarrassed phantom" of *Endymion,* held the office of Prime Minister without ever meeting Parliament.[3] The son was cast in a different mould from his wavering and impracticable father, who was in turn Tory, Whig, and Peelite. He started his own political career, in the company of Tom Hughes and Charles Kingsley, as a Christian Socialist, and an advanced Radical. During the seven years that he sat in the House of Commons (1852–1859) he formed a minute party of his own, which included Henry Bruce (Lord Aberdare) and W. E. Forster (not yet in the House) — both to become his colleagues in Mr. Gladstone's Administration of 1868 — who regarded Lord Palmerston and the Whigs as the incarnation of evil, and fell equally foul of the *laisser faire* of Cobden, and the peace doctrines of Bright. Ripon's hostility to Palmerston was gradu-

---

[3] He was one of the favourite butts of Cobbett, who nicknamed him "Prosperity Robinson" (after his Budget speech in 1825) and "Goody Goderich."

ally relaxed, and he joined his Government in 1859, first as Under Secretary, and then as Secretary of State for War. From that time onward he was regarded as an indispensable member of every Liberal Cabinet.[4] I myself have sat with him in four Cabinets, and though he had become a Roman Catholic of the ultramontane type, he continued to the end in politics to be a robust Liberal, with leanings to the Left. He was never a Whig.

Clarendon on the other hand never lost or watered down the Whig faith which he had adopted in his youth. As late as the end of 1858 he writes to his brother-in-law, Sir G. C. Lewis, also a Whig of the Whigs,[5] and then editor of the *Edinburgh Review*: —

I consider the Monarchy, the House of Lords, and the Established Church, as bound up together, and the whole as the most perfect of the various imperfections called Governments; so that I differ root and branch from Bright.

[Not that he was under any illusions as to the actual infirmities of his party.]

The Whigs, he writes, are in a very ragged state, but I believe you might rig them out in new uniforms and make them look decent for Parliament, by an article which should well pepper the Tories, and show how accurately the Whigs of 1832 estimated the requirements of the country, and the temper and character of the people; and that they can point to the long list of beneficial measures which they have since

---

[4] Except when he was sent to India as Governor General in 1880.

[5] Gladstone, who had been one of the severest critics of Lewis's finance, wrote of him when he died (1863): "A most able, most learned, most unselfish and most genial man, . . . with a noble and antique simplicity of character." — Morley, "Gladstone", II, 67.

carried, while the Tories can only point to their opposition to these measures, and to their falsified pre-
dictions of anarchy and spoliation twenty-eight years
ago.

It may be added that for the greater part of his
political life Mr. Gladstone was his typical *bête noire*
— the hall-mark in those days of the unadulterated
Whig. In the end, Clarendon and he became the
closest of colleagues and friends.

Clarendon was four times Foreign Secretary — in
the Coalition of Lord Aberdeen, in the patched-up
Administration of Lord Palmerston which followed,
in Lord Russell's short Government of 1865–1866,
and in Mr. Gladstone's first Cabinet in 1868. It may
be doubted whether any statesman has ever held that
office with more eminent qualifications. He soon had
the good fortune to find favour with Queen Victoria.[6]
Such was certainly the opinion of his last Chief with
whom he worked in complete cordiality. When he
died in June, 1870, Mr. Gladstone writes in his diary:
" An irreparable colleague, a statesman of many gifts,
a most lovable and genial man." Twenty years afterwards he told Lord Morley that of all the sixty-odd
colleagues with whom he had sat in the Cabinet, " the
very easiest and most attractive was Clarendon." [7]

In the distracted and vacillating Cabinet of Lord
Aberdeen, Clarendon was almost the only Minister

[6] " Letters ", 2d series, Vol. I, pp. 280, 310, 313, etc.
[7] Morley, " Gladstone ", III, 491. Mr. Gladstone was fond, in his
old age, of making this kind of review. He once told me which of these
sixty-odd gentlemen, who included the Duke of Wellington, he considered
" the most impossible."

who, throughout, kept a clear vision and a steady
head. It was he who first used the phrase, " we are
drifting towards war." [8] A few months earlier he had
written to G. C. Lewis: " I see little chance of avert-
ing war, which even in the most sacred cause is a
horrible calamity; but for such a cause as two sets of
barbarians quarrelling over a form of words, it is not
only shocking, but incredible." The actual origin of
that indefensible adventure, the Crimean War, could
not be more tersely or more accurately described.

It is to be remembered that the last great effort of
Clarendon's long career at the Foreign Office was an
endeavour to lay the foundation for a permanent
European peace. The aggressive wars which led in
the Sixties to the partition of the duchies, the humili-
ation and dismemberment of Austria, and the first
stages of German unity, had aroused the apprehen-
sions of great powers like France, and small powers
like Belgium and Holland. The competition in military preparations throughout the Continent was
already in full swing. France was searching right and
left for possible allies. In the autumn of 1869 Lord
Clarendon paid visits to Berlin and Paris. In both
capitals he used the plainest language. He spoke to
the statesmen and soldiers — to none with more urgency than to his old acquaintance, the Emperor
Napoleon III — of the " monster armaments, the intolerable burden imposed upon the peoples, and the
constant danger of war which they created." [9] On his

---

[8] In the House of Lords, February 14, 1854.
[9] Morley, " Gladstone ", II, 321.

return, having received some signs of encouragement from the French Foreign Minister, he proceeded to make overtures both to Prussia and to France for partial disarmament. He persisted tenaciously, with the hearty sympathy and coöperation of Mr. Gladstone, during the early months of 1870, and did not abandon the task until it became clear that success was hopeless. The main responsibility for its failure rests with Bismarck.

In 1871, a year after Clarendon's death, Odo Russell, who had married his daughter, became British Ambassador at Berlin. At some social function, Lady Emily fell into conversation with Count Bismarck, who suddenly said to her:

" Never in my life was I more glad to hear of anything than I was to hear of your father's death." Lady Emily was not unnaturally taken aback, whereupon Bismarck, patting her hand, said, " Ach, dear lady, you must not take it like that. What I mean is that, if your father had lived, he would have prevented the war." [10]

Such a tribute from such a quarter speaks for itself.

[10] This incident is taken from Sir H. Maxwell's interesting " Life of Clarendon ", II, 366.

CHAPTER III

MR. GLADSTONE'S COLLEAGUES (1869)

Lowe: Cardwell

ROBERT LOWE is a statesman of whom it is difficult to present a living picture, or to form a just and adequate estimate. His talents and accomplishments were of a very high order. He won great distinction in his youth both at Winchester and Oxford, where his career overlapped that of Gladstone and of Tait, and his name finds a place in the same First Class with those of the afterwards inseparable lexicographers, Liddell and Scott. He was also one of the leading speakers at the Union. After competing in vain for a professorship at Glasgow, he emigrated to Sydney, and was for some years a conspicuous and combative figure in the legal and political life of New South Wales. He returned to England with a competence, and in 1852 became a Member of the House of Commons, where he at once made his mark, and held a number of minor offices in successive Liberal Governments.

It was not till the controversy over Parliamentary Reform in 1866 and 1867, that he stepped into the front rank, with a series of speeches which can even now be read with more intellectual pleasure than those of any other contemporary orator. They breathe a genuine and outspoken hatred of the " arid plain " of democracy, where " every mole-hill is a mountain, and every thistle a forest-tree." The following passage from his denunciation of the Liberal Reform Bill of 1866 deserves to be disinterred from the graveyard of Hansard: [1]

I am not afraid of the people of this country. They have displayed a good sense which is remarkable, indeed, when contrasted with the harangues which have been addressed to them. But if I am not afraid of the people, neither do I agree with the Member for Huntingdon in fearing those by whom they are led. Demagogues are the commonplace of history. They are to be found wherever popular commotion has prevailed, and they all bear to one another a strong family likeness. Their names float lightly on the stream of time; they are in some way handed down to us, but then they are as little regarded as is the foam which rides on the crest of the stormy wave, and bespatters the rock which it cannot shake. Such men I do not fear, but I have, I confess, some misgivings when I see a number of gentlemen of rank, of character, of property, and intelligence, carried away, without being convinced or even over-persuaded, in the support of a policy which many of them in their inmost heart detest and abhor. Monarchies exist by loyalty, aristocracies by honour, popular assemblies by political virtue and patriotism, and it is in the loss of those things, and not in comets and eclipses, that we are to look for the portents that herald the fall of States.

I have said that I am utterly unable to reason with

[1] April 26, 1866.

the Chancellor of the Exchequer (Gladstone) for want of a common principle to start from. But there is happily one common ground left to us, and that is the second book of the Aeneid of Virgil. My right honourable friend, like the moth which has singed its wings in the candle, has returned again to the poor old Trojan horse; and I shall, with the permission of the House, give them one more excerpt from the history of that noble beast, first promising that I shall then turn him out to grass, at all events for the remainder of the session. The passage which I am about to quote is one which is, I think, worthy of the attention of the House, because it contains a description, not only of the invading army of which we have heard so much, but also a slight sketch of its general:

" Arduus armatos mediis in moenibus adstans
  Fundit equus, victorque Sinon incendia miscet
  Insultans: portis alii bipatentibus adsunt,
  Milia quot magnis umquam venere Mycenis."

In other words —

" The fatal horse pours forth the human tide,
  Insulting Sinon flings his firebrands wide,
  The gates are burst; the ancient rampart falls,
  And swarming millions climb its crumbling walls."

Surely the heroic work of so many centuries, the matchless achievements of so many wise heads and strong hands, deserve a nobler consummation than to be sacrificed at the shrine of revolutionary passion, or the maudlin enthusiasm of humanity! But if we do fall, we shall fall deservedly. Uncoerced by any external force, not borne down by any internal calamity; but in the full plethora of our wealth and the surfeit of our too exuberant prosperity, with our own rash and inconsiderate hands we are about to pluck down on our heads the venerable temple of our liberty and our glory. History may tell of other acts as signally disastrous, but of none more wanton, none more disgraceful.

It is instructive, in view of what happened afterwards, to recall that this magnificent invective was directed against a proposal to lower the occupation franchise, in boroughs to six pounds, and in counties to ten pounds. The following year (1867), when the Tory Government were engaged in carrying a measure for Household Suffrage, Lowe with perfect consistency altered the direction of his guns, and kept up an equally effective fusillade against Mr. Disraeli and his party for their " great betrayal." He never spoke so well in the remainder of his career.

Lowe was personally amiable as well as highly cultured, but a unique gift of sarcasm, coupled with an unlimited and unconcealed contempt for the stupidity of the average man,[2] are not qualities which endear a Parliamentarian to the House of Commons. Mr. Disraeli summed up, not only his own view, but probably that of many other members on both sides, in one of his incomparable sallies, the next year (1868), when Lowe had joined Mr. Gladstone's crusade against the Irish Church: " He (Lowe) is a very remarkable man. He is a learned man, though he despises history. He can chop logic like Dean Aldrich,

[2] There was in those days a highly respected member of the House of Commons who was deaf, and equipped himself with an ear trumpet. Lowe, seeing him use this implement in some dreary debate, remarked to his neighbour: " Why should a man throw away his natural advantages? "

but what is more remarkable than his learning and
his logic is that power of spontaneous aversion which
particularizes him. There is nothing that he likes,
and almost everything that he hates. He hates the
working classes of England. He hates the Roman
Catholics of Ireland. He hates the Protestants of Ireland. He hates Her Majesty's Ministers. And until
Mr. Gladstone placed his hand upon the ark, he
almost seemed to hate the right honourable gentleman.[3]

The selection by Mr. Gladstone of Lowe as Chancellor of the Exchequer in the new Cabinet — the
Trojan Horse having apparently been sent to the
stud — aroused more surprise and curiosity than any
of his other appointments. Lowe's tenure of that office coincided with a term of national prosperity, and
he was able to make substantial reductions both in
direct and indirect taxation. His finance was in essentials sound, though streaked by occasional vagaries,
such as his abortive match tax. But, largely through
defects of temperament and tact, he gradually became one of the most unpopular members of the
Administration. On the eve of its downfall (in the
autumn of 1873)[4] he exchanged the Exchequer for

[3] House of Commons, April 3, 1868.

[4] On the reconstruction of the Government, August, 1873, the Queen,
in a letter to Gladstone, asked: " Is it not very imprudent to put a
person who is so very unpopular as Mr. Lowe unfortunately is, into the
Home Office? " Granville wrote to Her Majesty: " Mr. Lowe is, of
course, the great stumbling-block. With ability almost amounting to
genius, he has faults of character and manner, which get him and his
colleagues into numerous scrapes. He is the culminating point of the
present difficulties, but with some exceptions he has been a very hard-
working, public-spirited servant of the Crown in his late office." —
" Letters of Queen Victoria ", II, 274. 1862–1878.

the Home Department, and after the catastrophe of January, 1874, through trivial and much exaggerated indiscretions, he was generally regarded as a source of weakness rather than of strength to his party. He never held office again, and after the great Liberal victory of 1880, took reluctant refuge in the House of Lords. He wrote to his brother (on the subject of his " elevation "):

" I have got again into the company of the four neuter verbs of the Latin Grammar: —

> Vapulo — I am beaten.
> Veneo — I am sold.
> Exulo — I am banished.
> Fio — I am done! " [5]

Mr. Gladstone, who was a far better judge of men than superficial critics were apt to suppose, wrote of Lowe (long afterwards): " In everything personal Lowe was an excellent colleague and Member of Cabinet, but full of contradictory qualities; splendid in attack, but most weak in defence . . . one day headstrong and independent, and the next helpless as a child to walk alone; capable of tearing anything to pieces, but of constructing nothing." [6] And in a letter to Lowe himself (while they were still colleagues) he says: " You see everything in a burning, almost a scorching light. . . . Outstripping others in the race, you reach the goal or conclusion before them, and being there you assume that they are there

[5] " Life of Lord Sherbrooke ", by A. P. Martin, II, 441.
[6] " Hamilton ", Monograph, p. 32.

also. This is unpopular. . . . Again, I think you do
not get up all things, but allow yourself a choice, as
if politics were a flower garden and we might choose
among the beds; as Lord Palmerston did, who read
Foreign Office and War papers, and let the others rust
and rot. This I think is partially true, I do not say
of your reading, but of your mental processes." [7]

Few Prime Ministers have shown more penetrating
and relentless candour to the most brilliant of their
colleagues.

The once famous epitaph on Lowe is worth res-
cuing from oblivion. Some anonymous correspondent
sent him towards the end of his official career the
following lines:

> " Here lie the bones of Robert Lowe
> Where he's gone to I don't know:
> If to the realms of peace and love
> Farewell to happiness above:
> If, haply, to some lower level,
> We can't congratulate the Devil."

Lowe showed them to Mr. Gladstone, who
promptly furnished a Latin version:

> " Roberti Lowe hic corpus jacet
> Qua sit ipse, Musa tacet:
> Ad superna si volabit,
> Pax e caelis exulabit;
> Sin an inferos meabit
> Et Diabolum vexabit."

W. E. G., July 18, 1873.

[7] Morley, " Gladstone ", II, 464–465.

Lowe's own version of the last lines is perhaps even more felicitous:

" Si caelum scandet ista pestis
Vale! concordia caelestis;
Sin apud inferos jacebit,
Diabolum ejus poenitebit,
Et nos Diaboli miserebit."

R. L., March 18, 1873.[8]

Edward Cardwell, who was a contemporary of Lowe at Oxford, where he had an equally distinguished career, was endowed with less brilliant gifts, but has left a much more enduring mark both in legislation and in administration. He was a man after Sir Robert Peel's own heart, and it was by Peel that he was introduced and trained to official life. With the other Peelites he gravitated to the Liberal side, and both at the Board of Trade and the Colonial Office he did admirable work, particularly in the promotion of self-defence and self-government in the Colonies. He put an end to transportation, and laid down the lines upon which Canadian Confederation was carried out by his successors. Mr. Gladstone called him to the War Office in 1868, and the achievement with which his name will always be associated was the re-organization of the British Army, of which the leading features were the abolition of purchase, the introduction of short service, and the formation of a reserve. Never, until the advent to the same office of Mr. Haldane in 1905, had a civilian Minister a more for-

---

[8] " Life of Lord Sherbrooke ", II, 410–411.

midable task, and Cardwell brought to its accomplish-
ment a complete mastery both of principle and detail,
an infinite fund of patience, unfailing tact, and the
most resolute courage. His active public life came to
an end in 1874, when he went to the House of Lords.

In 1867 several of the English Liberal leaders
happened to be in Rome at the same time, and had
interviews with the Pope, Pius IX. According to Mr.
Gladstone's report,[9] the Pope summarized his impres-
sions of them as follows:

" I like but do not understand Mr. Gladstone;
Mr. Cardwell I understand, but I do not like; I both
like and understand Lord Clarendon; the Duke of
Argyle I neither understand nor like."

Bishop Wilberforce speaks of Cardwell's " medita-
tive, introverted, susceptible spirit." Lord Selborne,
who had known him since their schooldays at Winchester, writes of him that " he changed his own
opinion less, from first to last, than any man of equal
ability and independence of mind whom I ever knew.
He always knew his own mind; and was at all points
and in all things a true man; in private life, as in
public, spotless; and a most faithful friend." [10]

---

[9] Morley, " Gladstone ", II, 218.   [10] Memorials, II, 244.

CHAPTER IV

PARLIAMENTARY ELOQUENCE IN 1869

NO one now takes much interest in the details of
the Irish Church Bill, or in the adjustment of the
differences arising out of it between the two Houses,
which was largely due to the tact and skill of Queen
Victoria herself. Mr. Gladstone's conduct of the Bill
through the House of Commons remains to this day
an almost unexampled parliamentary achievement.
He was then at the very top of his powers. The pilot-
ing of a complicated and highly technical measure
through the Committee of the whole House always
has been as severe a test as can be devised, both of
capacity and temperament. Mr. Gladstone bore the
whole burden, and was more than equal to the task.
The only parallel case was supplied by himself,
twelve years later, in his conduct of the Irish Land
Bill of 1881.

The debates in both Houses were made remarkable by some of the best efforts of the famous speakers of the time; and it may not be amiss in these days
when what Byron calls the " Pedestrian Muses " are
in fashion, to give some specimens of the art of
oratory, as it was understood and practised fifty
years ago, by its most accomplished and experienced
masters.

Take first the following passages from Mr. Bright's speech on the second reading of the Irish Church Bill in the House of Commons:

" I said, many years ago, and I repeat it now, that by the policy which England has pursued in Ireland, we have made Catholicism not a faith only to which people cling with a desperate and heroic tenacity, but a patriotism for which multitudes of her children are willing to suffer, and, if necessary, to die. And what should be more likely than that, because this State Church, this Protestant ascendancy, has been for three centuries leagued with every form of injustice of which the Irish people have complained, whether connected with the confiscation of their soil, or with the terrors and cruelties of the odious Penal Code, or with the administration of the law, or with any social tyranny to which they have been subjected? Has the Church done anything to bind Ireland to Great Britain? For centuries, we all know, Ireland has been restless, turbulent and insurrectionary. . . . If we come down to the seventy years during which this House has governed Ireland, we find things much in the same way. The pages of her history have been stained with tears and blood. There have still been restlessness and turbulence and insurrection appearing and reappearing constantly on the records of her sad and dismal story. Mr. Gathorne Hardy referred last session to the Church in Ireland as the light of the Reformation. He appeared not able to comprehend that this light of the Reformation, sustained by privilege, and fanned as it has been by the hot breath of faction, has been not so much a helpful light as a scorching fire, which has burned up almost everything good and noble in the country, and industry and charity and peace and loyalty have perished in its flames.

" If I were particular on the point as to the sacred nature of the endowments, I should even then be satisfied with the propositions in this Bill — for, after all, I hope it is not far from Christianity to charity; and we know that the Divine Founder of our faith has left much more of the doings of a compassionate and loving heart than He has a dogma. . . . Do you not think that from the charitable dealing with these matters even a sweeter incense may arise than when those vast funds are applied to maintain three times the number of clergy than can be of the slightest use to the Church with which they are connected? We can do but little, it is true. We cannot relume the extinguished lamp of reason. We cannot make the deaf to hear. We cannot make the dumb to speak. It is not given to us:

' From the thick film to purge the visual ray,
And on the sightless eyeballs pour the day.'

But at least we can lessen the load of affliction, and we can make life more tolerable to vast numbers who suffer."

I know nothing finer in the annals of British eloquence.

By way of pendant, contrast the following, spoken on the same Bill in the opposite sense, by the veteran

Lord Derby in the House of Lords. It is from the last, and in the opinion of so competent a judge as Mr. Saintsbury, almost the greatest, of his speeches. Lord Derby (Mr. Saintsbury tells us) " like all good men ", was a devotee of Sir Walter Scott. But what parliamentary speaker now, in either House, would venture upon a quotation of some twenty lines of " Guy Mannering? "

" My Lords, I may venture upon an illustration of a very simple kind with which all your lordships are probably acquainted, and which none of your lordships can have heard without having been touched by its simple pathos. The language represents the feelings of a poor gipsy, when she and her tribe were driven out from the homes in which they had for many years found a shelter — driven out by a man to whom they had long looked for protection, a protection which they had repaid by the most affectionate devotion. ' Ride your ways, Laird of Ellangowan; ride your ways, Godfrey Bertram! This day have ye quenched seven smoking hearths — see if the fire in your ain parlour burn the blither for that. Ye have riven the thack off seven cottar houses — look if your ain roof-tree stand the faster. . . . There's thirty hearts there that wad hae wanted bread ere ye had wanted sunkets, and spent their life blood ere ye had scratched your finger.'

" My Lords, it is with sentiments like these — with sorrow, but with resentment — that the Protestants of Ireland may look upon you from whom they expected protection — a protection which they repaid with the most faithful loyalty, when they now find you laying upon them the heavy hand of what I must consider an undeserved oppression. They may say, ' Go your ways, Ministers of England, ye have this day, as far as in you lay, quenched the light of spiritual truth in fifteen hundred parishes. See if your own Church stands the faster for that.' There are not seven nor thirty, but 700,000 hearts, and 700,000 more, who have connected themselves with you in loyal attachment to the Sovereign for the sake of that Protestant religion you both profess, who, in defence of that union which you induced them to form, would have shed their dearest life blood. Remember who these men are. These are the men whom you invited to settle on the soil of Ireland for the establishment and support of the Protestant religion. These are the men who, at the time of the sorest trial of the Crown of England, came forward to support William the Deliverer, and who, at the battle of Boyne, vindicated the freedom of Ireland and the rights of the Protestant religion. These are the men who, invited by you to settle in Ireland, converted Ulster from a barren waste into a thriving province, and who, by their energy, their industry, and their steady conduct, have made the province of Ulster not merely the garden of Ireland, but the most gratifying and wonderful contrast to those parts of Ireland in which the Protestant religion does not prevail."

It was in these debates that a newcomer from Ireland first addressed the House of Lords, in which, up to the time of his death, he certainly had no superior either in wit or in eloquence. This was Magee, who had been for some years Dean of Cork, and whom the Queen described in a letter to Mr. Disraeli (September, 1868) as the " finest speaker she had ever heard out of Scotland." In a general shuffle of ecclesiastical prizes, which took place in the last month of Disraeli's year of office, Magee had asked not to be forgotten, and obtained by Her Majesty's insistence, with the reluctant assent of the Prime Minister, the Bishopric of Peterborough.[2] His maiden speech on the second reading, June 15, 1869, created a profound impression, which a perusal of it in cold blood after fifty years may hardly seem fully to justify. He warned the Peers not to yield to the menaces which were being so freely addressed to them both from without and within. If they should give way, what would be the consequence?

" You would then be standing in the face of a fierce and angry democracy with these words on your lips: ' Spare us, we entreat and beseech you! Spare us to live a little longer as an Order, is all that we ask — so that we may play at being statesmen, that we may sit upon red benches in a gilded house, and affect and pretend to guide the destinies of the nation. Spare us, for this reason — that we are utterly con-temptible and that we are entirely contented with our ignoble position! Spare us, for this reason — that we have never failed in any case of danger to spare our-selves! Spare us, because we have lost the power to hurt any one! Spare us, because we have now become

[2] Buckle, " Disraeli ", V, pp. 64–67.

the mere subservient tools in the hands of the Minister of the day, the mere armorial bearings on the seal that he may take in his hands to stamp any deed, however foolish and however mischievous. And this is all we have to say by way of plea for the continuance of our Order.' "

CHAPTER V

1868–1873

THE legislative output of the Government progressed with unabated fertility. Mr. Bright, who had *au fond* strong Conservative instincts, protested in vain that it was not " easy to drive six omnibuses abreast through Temple Bar." The session of 1870 was made memorable by the first of Mr. Gladstone's Irish Land Acts, and by the Education Act for England and Wales, which were followed in subsequent sessions by the establishment of Secret Voting, the abolition of Purchase in the Army, and of University Tests, and the removal of the Civil Disabilities of Trade Unions. The Irish Land Act, though devised with the best intentions, and with much ingenuity and skill, did not go to the root of agrarian discontent. The Education Act, which was in all essentials the handiwork of one of the younger Ministers, W. E. Forster, provoked the bitter hostility of a large and loyal section of the Liberal rank and file, the Nonconformists, which found a centre and rallying point at Birmingham, under a new leader not yet in Parliament — Joseph Chamberlain — and became the largest contributory cause of the overwhelming defeat of the party at the general election of 1874. Mr.

Chamberlain had as his most powerful ally a new associate, who, though still, and for many years after, outside the House of Commons, was already a considerable figure in the literary world — John Morley. It was in some ways an incongruous partnership, but it became a very effective one, and survived many strains, until it reached — through what may be called a mischance in the chapter of accidents — its breaking point over the Home Rule Bill of 1886. How acrimonious the estrangement of the stalwart Radicals from Mr. Gladstone caused by the controversy over education had become, may be judged from a passage in one of Morley's articles in the *Fortnightly Review*, of which he was then editor:

" Mr. Disraeli," he wrote, " had the satisfaction of dishing the Whigs, who were his enemies. Mr. Gladstone, on the other hand, dished the Dissenters, who were his friends. Unfortunately, he omitted one element of prime importance in these rather nice transactions. He forgot to educate his party."

In the same spirit Chamberlain appealed to the Nonconformists to withhold support at elections from Liberals, " until they learned the Liberal alphabet, and could spell the first words of the Liberal Cause."

The tide of popularity had already begun to ebb in 1872. Mr. Disraeli was only waiting his opportunity, and the revival of an aggressive and militant Opposition may be said to date from two famous speeches made by him in that year — the one at Manchester in April, the other at the Crystal Palace in June. They are worth more than a passing notice, for they supplied his party for years to come with dialectical and rhetorical pabulum.

The Manchester speech was made in the Free Trade Hall, and its delivery occupied three and a quarter hours. His main theme was the debt due by the country to its fundamental institutions — the Monarchy, the House of Lords, the Established Church — of which the Tory Party were the natural custodians, and which, one after another, were being openly attacked, or insidiously undermined, by the Radicals. He urged his followers, however, not to be content with the defence of these ancient citadels, but to advance boldly, in search of working class support, into the field of Social Reform. He even supplied them with a Latin motto for this new crusade: *Sanitas sanitatum, omnia Sanitas.* " After all, the first consideration of a Minister should be the health of the people." And in an immortal passage, he held up to ridicule the plight of an overwrought and worn-out Government, whose " paroxysms had ended in prostration: "

" As I sat opposite the Treasury Bench, the Ministers reminded me of one of those marine landscapes not very unusual on the coasts of South America. You behold a range of exhausted volcanoes. Not a flame flickers on a single pallid crest. But the situation is still dangerous. There are occasional earthquakes, and ever and anon the dark rumbling of the sea."

The effect of this speech (one of his happiest efforts) was enormous. Even so cool-headed and

phlegmatic a critic as Lord Cairns became enthusiastic. " It will live and be read," he wrote to Disraeli,
" not only for its sparkling vigour, but also for the
deep strata of constitutional thought and reasoning
which pervade it." [1]

A couple of months later (June 24) Disraeli followed up this deliverance by a speech at the Crystal
Palace, in which he amplified his Manchester programme. It was then that he first discovered, or at
any rate first disclosed, the British Empire as an
electoral asset of the Tory Party. It is not, perhaps,
fair to lay undue stress on what his biographer apolo-
getically describes as a " petulant outburst ", in a
letter to a colleague in Lord Derby's first Ministry
twenty years earlier: " These wretched Colonies will
all be independent, too, in a few years, and are a
millstone round our necks." [2] But as lately as 1866,
being once more Chancellor of the Exchequer, he had
written to the Prime Minister, Lord Derby: " Power
and influence we should exercise in Asia; consequently in Eastern Europe; consequently also in
Western Europe; but what is the use of these colonial
deadweights which we do not govern? " [3]

The gospel proclaimed at the Crystal Palace was in
a very different key. One or two of its salient points
deserve (if only for their supreme audacity of statement) textual citation:

" If you look to the history of this country since
the advent of Liberalism — forty years ago — you
will find that there has been no effort so continuous,

[1] Buckle, "Disraeli ", V, 190.   [2] *Ibid.*, III, 385.   [3] *Ibid.*, IV, 476.

so subtle, supported by so much energy, and carried on with so much ability and acumen, as the attempts of Liberalism to effect the disintegration of the Empire of England. And of all its efforts this is the one which has been nearest success. . . . It has been proved to all of us that we have lost money by our colonies. It has been shown with precise, with mathematical demonstration, that there never was a jewel in the Crown of England that was so truly costly as the possession of India. How often has it been suggested that we should at once emancipate ourselves from this incubus! Well, that result was nearly accomplished. *When those subtle views were adopted by the country under the plausible plea of granting self-government to the Colonies, I confess that I myself thought that the tie was broken."*

He went on to urge that self-government, when it was " conceded ", ought to have been accompanied by an Imperial Tariff; by securities " for the people of England for the enjoyment of the unappropriated lands which belonged to the Sovereign as their trustee "; by a military code; and by the institution of a representative Council in the Metropolis. And his final conclusion was that " no Minister in this country will do his duty who neglects any opportunity of reconstructing as much as possible our Colonial Empire." For this sacred task the Conservatives would find inspiration and support in the " sublime instincts of an ancient people." [4]

The actual course of Conservative policy, during

4 Buckle, " Disraeli ", V, 194–196.

the remaining ten years of Disraeli's life, is a sufficient commentary upon the sincerity of this strange compound of distorted history and stilted rhetoric.

Troubles and worries, great and small, continued to accumulate for the Liberal Government. The arbitration between Great Britain and the United States over the " Alabama " claims " hung ", as the Speaker records, " like a cloud over the proceedings in Parliament "; and the ultimate award of over three millions was accepted as a disagreeable necessity. The failure of the Irish University Bill was a serious blow to the prestige of the Ministry. Two trumpery matters, the so-called Collier and Ewelme " scandals " , in which Mr. Gladstone was personally involved, were inflated into affairs of national importance; and when, upon the reconstruction of the Cabinet in the autumn of 1873, he accepted in addition to the Prime Ministership the office of Chancellor of the Exchequer, without seeking reëlection to the House of Commons, there was, notwithstanding a wide divergence of legal opinion, further occasion for misunderstanding and prejudice.

Meanwhile Mr. Disraeli, who had astutely refused to take office when Mr. Gladstone resigned over the collapse of the Irish University Bill in the spring of 1873, continued to make the most of the situation in the interests of his own party. If he may seem to fastidious critics of a later time to have forced the note, and more than once to have passed the limit of good taste and even of good sense, he knew (as the event proved) what he was about.

Early in October, 1873, there was a by-election at Bath, and in a letter to the party candidate, Lord Grey de Wilton, the Tory leader wrote as follows:

For nearly five years the present Ministers have harassed every trade, worried every profession, and assailed or menaced every class, institution, and species of property in the country. Occasionally they have varied this state of civil warfare by perpetrating some job which outraged public opinion, or by stumbling into mistakes which have been always discreditable and sometimes ruinous. All this they call a policy and seem quite proud of it; but the country has, I think, made up its mind to close this career of *plundering and blundering.*[5]

The letter failed of its immediate purpose, for Lord Grey de Wilton was beaten at the polls; but Disraeli, far from quailing before the storm of criticism which it had let loose, writes to one of his nearest friends: " I wished to give a condensed but strictly accurate summary of the career of the Gladstone Ministry. There is not an expression which was not well-weighed, and which I could not justify by ample and even abounding evidence." [6]

A month later (November, 1873) he went to Glasgow to be installed as Lord Rector of the University, and to receive the freedom of the city. He had a tumultuous and enthusiastic reception. Two characteristic utterances may be cited from his address to the local Conservatives:

[5] A phrase borrowed from " Coningsby." See Buckle, " Disraeli ", V, 262.

[6] *Ibid.,* V, 263.

" It may be the proud destiny of England to guard civilization alike from the withering blast of Atheism and from the simoom of sacerdotal usurpation." And he warned the people of Scotland to " leave off mumbling the dry bones of political economy, and munching the remainder biscuit of an effete Liberalism."

Disraeli was now on the verge of seventy; he had had to wait a long time for the supreme opportunity; but he never failed in patience or in courage. His hour had come.

Parliament was dissolved in January, 1874. The general election resulted in a Conservative majority of one hundred over the Liberals, and of about fifty over Liberals and Home Rulers combined. Mr. Gladstone resigned, and Mr. Disraeli became, for the second time, Prime Minister.

CHAPTER VI

1874–1875: MR. GLADSTONE'S RETIREMENT

IN the Cabinet of twelve there was only one new man — Cross — whose appointment was a recognition of the electoral debt which the Conservatives owed to Lancashire; he proved himself a very capable Home Secretary. The other feature of interest in its personnel was the accession of Lord Salisbury. For many years he had been barely on speaking terms with his Chief, and when, during the formation of the Government, he was being pressed by his friends to take office, he wrote to his wife that " the prospect of having to serve with this man again is like a nightmare." He was in time to become Disraeli's most intimate and trusted colleague.

The House of Commons elected in 1874 was afterwards described by Gladstone as the " most reactionary, the most apathetic, and the least independent " in which he ever sat. Whether or not these disparaging epithets were justified, there can be no doubt that the mandate it had received from the electors was a mandate of Tranquillity.

In it were to be found two notable newcomers: " Captain " A. J. Balfour (who, it appears, held a commission in the East Lothian and Berwickshire

Militia), and Lord Randolph Churchill.[1] They were joined in the course of the next two years by two equally remarkable recruits — Charles Stewart Parnell and Joseph Chamberlain. It may be doubted whether any other House of Commons has witnessed the début of four men who were destined, in diverse ways, to exercise such a dominating influence both in debate and in policy. It was memorable also for the appearance for the first time of a separately organized Home Rule Party under the leadership of Isaac Butt, and of two Miners' members — Burt and Macdonald — who for political and party purposes were still numbered in the Liberal ranks.

The Liberals were not only in a minority, but very soon found themselves without a leader.

Mr. Gladstone, at the final meeting of his Cabinet, had declared to his colleagues that he should not retain the leadership, but sit as a private member. He was persuaded by them to defer for a time the public announcement of his intentions. Curiously enough, one of the considerations by which he seems to have been genuinely influenced was that of age. A few months before (May, 1873) Bishop Wilberforce reports a conversation with him on the subject: " Gladstone talking much how little real good work

---

[1] Mr. Disraeli's comment (in a letter to Queen Victoria, May 22, 1874) on Lord R. Churchill's maiden speech, is worth recalling: — " Lord Randolph said many imprudent things which is not very important in the maiden speech of a young member and a young man; but the House was surprised, and then captivated by his energy, and natural flow, and his impressive manner. With self-control and study he might mount." A good example of Disraeli's insight and prescience in the judgment of men.

THE RIGHT HON. WILLIAM EWART
GLADSTONE

any Premier had done after sixty," citing the cases of
Peel, Palmerston, and Wellington. And a day or two
later: " Gladstone again talking of sixty as full age
of Premier." In the spring of 1874 he had already
exceeded this limit by nearly five years, and the gods
had decreed that he was to be three times again
Prime Minister, once at the age of seventy-one, again
when he was seventy-seven, and finally when he was
eighty-three.

Many years afterwards (1882) when Mr. Gladstone was in the full blast of the political storms
which, blowing in from every quarter, disturbed and
indeed distracted his second premiership, the Metro-
politan See of Canterbury became vacant. It was the
opinion of the Archbishop (Tait) whose death caused
the vacancy, and (very strongly) of Queen Victoria,
that his proper successor was Harold Browne, the
Bishop of Winchester. Mr. Gladstone shared their
estimate of the Bishop's preëminent claims, but
(being himself seventy-three years of age) vetoed the
appointment because Doctor Browne was already
seventy-one. His letter to the disappointed Prelate
is so Gladstonian as to be worth quoting:

It may seem strange that I, who, in my own person, exhibit so conspicuously the anomaly of a dis-
parate conjunction between years and duties, should
be thus forward in interpreting the circumstances of
another case, certainly more mitigated in many respects, yet differing from my own case in one vital
point, the newness of the duties of the English, or
rather Anglican or British Primacy, to a Diocesan

Bishop however able and experienced, and the newness of mental attitude and action which they would
require. Among the materials of judgment in such an
instance it seems right to reckon precedents for what
they are worth.

He cannot find an instance of a man of seventy
being appointed to Canterbury, since the time of
Sheldon. Bishop Browne writes to a friend à propos
of this search for precedents: " Curiously I have been
reading that he (Gladstone) himself, prompted by
Bishop Wilberforce, wanted Palmerston to appoint
Sumner of Winchester when he was 72." [2]

Newman remarks at the close of his correspondence with Manning, in which the two future Car-
dinals interchange the promise of Masses for each
other's intention: [3] " I do not know whether I am on
my head or my heels when I have active relations
with you."

It is perhaps not a matter of surprise that hostile
critics, both at the time and since, declared that the
whole thing was nothing but a pose. It is one of the
many paradoxes, in the complicated temperament
and character of this illustrious man, that, with an
almost unrivalled faculty of lucid and convincing
statement, he took what seems like a perverse pleasure from time to time in saying and writing things
which puzzled and baffled plain people. One of the
most characteristic cases is the manner in which he
dealt with his singularly unhappy speech during the

[2] Morley, " Gladstone ", III, 95–96.
[3] Purcell, " Life of Manning ", II, 341, 346.

American Civil War (1862), when he declared that
" Jefferson Davis and the other leaders of the South
have made an Army; they are making, it appears, a
Navy; and they have made what is more than either,
they have made a Nation." This was almost universally construed as meaning that the British Government was about to recognize the independence
of the South. In the storm of criticism which was
aroused, he thought it sufficient to direct his Secretary to write as follows: " Mr. Gladstone desires me
to remark that to form opinions upon questions of
policy, to announce them to the world, and to take,
or to be a party to taking, any of the steps necessary
for giving them effect, are matters which, though connected together, are in themselves distinct, and which
may be separated by intervals of time, longer or
shorter, according to the particular circumstances of
the case." [4]

Another illustration is to be found in his dicta in
1880 and 1881 on the annexation of the Transvaal.
Speaking before the election at Peebles on March 30,
1880, of the Transvaal and Cyprus, he said: " If
those acquisitions were as valuable as they are value-
less, I would repudiate them, because they are obtained by means dishonourable to the character of
our country." Taxed with this language, when after
coming into office he had resolved to maintain the
annexation of the Transvaal, his explanation in the
House of Commons (January 21, 1881) was that
" repudiate " at Peebles meant " disapprove ", and

4 Morley, " Gladstone ", II, 79–80.

that to disapprove of the annexation of a country is one thing: to abandon that annexation is another." [5]

Even his intimate colleagues were sometimes left in perplexity as to his real meaning. Thus we find Lord Hartington writing to Lord Granville in August, 1885: " I never can understand Mr. Gladstone in conversation, and I thought him unusually unintelligible yesterday.[6]

There is no real reason to suppose that in 1874 he was playing a part. Politics for the time being had ceased to interest him: he could not see in them, at the moment and in the near future, any " work of noble note ", " not unbecoming men that strove with Gods." A hundred other interests on which he could well expend his time and strength, up to the limits of the ordinary span of mortality, called to him with insistent and divergent appeals. More than twenty years afterwards, he says, " I deeply desired an interval between Parliament and the grave."

And at the time he writes to Mrs. Gladstone with obvious sincerity: " I am convinced that the welfare of mankind does not now depend on the State or the world of politics: the real battle is being fought in the world of thought, where a deadly attack is made, with great tenacity of purpose, over a wide field, upon the greatest treasure of mankind, the belief in God and the gospel of Christ." [7] And, a year later, in a somewhat different vein: " For the general business

---

[5] " Life of Devonshire ", I, 237.
[6] *Ibid.*, II, 77.
[7] Morley, " Gladstone ", II, 500.

of the country, my ideas and temper are thoroughly
out of harmony with the ideas and temper of the
day." [8] Happily for himself he found a completely
congenial outlet for his still more than ample reser-
voir of combative energy, in the controversy with
the Ultramontanes over the Vatican Decrees, to
which he devoted the autumn of 1874. " I pass my
days and nights (he writes in December) in the
Vatican."

Without any definite and formal abdication his
attendance in the House of Commons in its first
session had become uncertain and irregular. It was
only when some ecclesiastical matter like the Public
Worship Regulation Bill " to put down Ritualism "
came up for discussion that his interests were aroused,
and he threw himself into the fray. On the Front
Bench, on which sat Hartington, Goschen, Forster,
Lowe, there was no one with commanding authority;
in Mr. Bright's words, there was " no one leading —
no one yielding — only chaos." A situation which
had become intolerable was put an end to by Gladstone's publicly announced retirement at the beginning of the session of 1875. He continued when he
came to the House to sit side by side with Bright on
the Front Opposition Bench.

There was no eagerness among his late colleagues
(in Lord Fitzmaurice's phrase) to " play Addington
to his Pitt " : for not a few of them were sceptical as
to the finality of the step which he had taken. There
were, in the end, only two effective competitors for

the unenvied post, each of whom would have gladly yielded it to the other: Hartington and Forster. Forster, to whom the more Radical section of the party would naturally have inclined, was still the *bête noire* of the Nonconformists, and Hartington was selected as the man who would divide the party the least. Disraeli, in a familiar letter, with sardonic good nature, describes his maiden speech in his new part as " sensible, dullish, and gentlemanlike." Lowe's comment upon it was equally characteristic: " At last I have heard a proper leader's speech: all good sense and no earnest nonsense." [9] Modest as were the expectations of the new leader formed both by his opponents and by his party, and by no one more sincerely than by himself, Hartington — in a position of exceptional difficulty — for no one could ever tell upon what occasion, or for what purpose, or in what mood, " the great Achilles " might emerge from his tent [10] — was not long in showing that he was a man to reckon with.

The session of 1875, though it had one or two tempestuous episodes — such as the outburst of Mr. Plimsoll and its consequences — was the last spell of tranquillity in the troubled years of the Disraeli-Beaconsfield Government. It produced a useful, though not ambitious, crop of social and industrial legislation: the first instalment of the " *Sanitas Sanitatum* " policy.

[9] Buckle, " Disraeli ", V, 362.
[10] One of the most curious of these intermittent forays was occasioned by the excellent proposal in Sir S. Northcote's Budget of 1875 to set up the New Sinking Fund. Buckle, " Disraeli ", V, 377-378.

The Prime Minister's eyes, however, were directed to wider horizons, and it was in the autumn of this year that he hazarded his first *coup* in the domain of foreign policy — the purchase of the Khedive's interest in the Suez Canal. The story has been often told, and need not be repeated here. But apart from the merits or drawbacks of the transaction, it is interesting as the first illustration of the divergence, in temperament and point of view, between Disraeli and his Foreign Secretary, Lord Derby, which had so much to do with the curves of British policy during the next three years. They had hitherto worked together in complete mutual confidence for the best part of thirty years. In a private letter, written to Derby by Disraeli at the moment of his own retirement from the House of Commons (August, 1876), he concludes as follows: — " Adieu! *cher camarade!* I wish you success and fame — and believe you will obtain both; but in great affairs, to succeed you must not spare the feelings of mediocrities." [11]

[11] Buckle, " Disraeli ", VI, 48.

CHAPTER VII

1876–1878

THE opening of the year 1876 was signalized by the introduction of a Royal Titles Bill to authorize the Queen to assume, in addition to her other titles, that of Empress of India. The measure was opposed by all the Liberal leaders, and by none of them with more vehemence than Mr. Gladstone: as Disraeli complained, " with unrivalled powers of casuistry." It was the last session in Mr. Disraeli's long membership of the House of Commons, and he found in the defence of the new title a thoroughly congenial topic for some of his farewell contributions to the debates of the Assembly, which he had so long adorned, and to which his removal was an impoverishing loss.

He recalled the happiness of the Roman world in the age of the Antonines: " and the Antonines were Emperors." " The amplification of titles is no new system — no new idea; [1] it has marked all ages, and has been in accordance with the manners and customs of all countries. . . . It is only by the amplifications of titles that you can often touch and satisfy the imagination of nations; and that is an element which Governments must not despise."

[1] I believe that the Emperor Charles V had seventy-five titles.

One of the objections taken was that in the " amplified " title the Colonies were not included. Mr. Disraeli distinguished their case from that of India on the ground of their fluctuating and impermanent populations. It is possible that some of his expressions might jar in these days upon the ears of our more full-blooded Imperialists; but it is quite likely that the orator had his tongue in his cheek.

" A Colonist finds a nugget or he fleeces a thousand flocks. He makes a fortune, he returns to England, he buys an estate. He becomes a Magistrate, he represents Majesty, he becomes High Sheriff. He has a magnificent house near Hyde Park; he goes to Court, to levees, to drawing-rooms; he has an opportunity of plighting his troth personally to the Sovereign, he is in frequent and direct communication with Her Majesty." [2]

Perhaps as bizarre an argument as has ever been used.

On Friday, August 11, 1876, Disraeli, without any formal farewell, left the precincts of the House (as Dilke records) " in a long white overcoat, and dandified lavender kid gloves, leaning on his Secretary's arm." Next morning it was announced that he had been created Earl of Beaconsfield. Recurrent attacks of gout, and the growing burden of protracted sittings in the House, where he was up to the end punctiliously regular in his attendance, compelled him to follow the example of the Great Commoner of the Eighteenth Century. He appointed, as his successor

[2] House of Commons, March 9, 1876.

in the leadership of the House, Sir Stafford North-cote.

The House of Commons became a different and much duller place when, of its two greatest figures, one was permanently withdrawn, and the other had become a fitful and erratic visitor.

As Sir W. Harcourt wrote in a farewell letter to the new peer: " Henceforth the game will be like a chessboard when the Queen is gone — a petty struggle of Pawns."

Years afterwards, a few months before his death, Lord Beaconsfield is reported to have said to Sir Henry Wolff:

" When Mr. Gladstone announced his withdrawal from public life I fully believed his statement, which was confirmed to me from special sources in which I placed the most implicit reliance. I thought that when he was gone Northcote would be able to cope with any one likely to assume the lead on the other side, and I wanted rest. I now much regret having retired from the House of Commons, as Mr. Gladstone, contrary to my firm persuasion, returned." [3]

At the time when Disraeli left the House of Commons the " Eastern Question ", which absorbed not only British, but European politics for the next two years, was already in full blast. It is no part of my purpose to rewrite its history. The ground has been completely covered by the biographies of Gladstone,

[3] " Lord Randolph Churchill ", by the Rt. Hon. W. S. Churchill, 1907 ed., in one vol., p. 127.

Disraeli, and the other statesmen of those days. I shall merely refer to it in some of its parliamentary and personal aspects.

It provoked the final encounter on the floor of the House between the two old antagonists, and the watchwords which they then appropriated — the " Concert of Europe " on the one side, and " British Interests " on the other — became the rallying cries of their partisans throughout the country.

Disraeli's policy was summed up in his last speech in the House of Commons. " Those," he said, " who suppose that England ever would uphold, or at this particular moment is upholding, Turkey from blind superstition, and from a want of sympathy with the highest aspirations of humanity, are deceived. What our duty is at this critical moment is to maintain the Empire of England. Nor will we ever agree to any step, though it may obtain for a moment comparative quiet and a false prosperity, that hazards the existence of that Empire."

In the seething turmoil which followed, party ties were severely strained. " Hartington," writes his biographer, " always suspicious of the poetical, disliked the exaggerated language of Tory speakers about the British Empire and British interests and British prestige. He disliked still more the perpetual attack made by Gladstonian speakers upon the doctrine that British statesmen must be guided by British interests. . . . The passionate agitation led in letters and speeches by Mr. Gladstone during the autumn of 1876, and actively supplied with fuel for

its flames from Nonconformist [and High Church]
pulpits and Radical platforms, was distasteful to
him." [4] Chamberlain and the Radicals began to
clamour for the restoration of Gladstone to the
leadership. But this was not the opinion of Mr.
Bright, and still less of Sir W. Harcourt, who expressed his view of the situation with his wonted
pungency in a letter to Dilke (October, 1876).[5]

Things here are in the most damnable mess, that
I think politics have ever been in my time. Gladstone and Dizzy seem to cap one another in folly and
imprudence, and I don't know which has made the
greatest ass of himself. . . . Chamberlain and Faw-
cett and the extreme crew are using the opportunity
to demand the demission of Hartington and the return of Gladstone. But you need not be alarmed, or
prepare for extreme measures. There is no fear of a
return from Elba. He is *played out*. His recent conduct has made all sober people more than ever distrust him. He has done two good things: he has
damaged the Government much, and himself still
more. At both of which I am pleased, and most of all
at the last.

Things reached a climax when, in April, 1877,
Gladstone, without the approval of a single one of
his old colleagues, gave notice of his famous Five
Resolutions in the House of Commons. Any one who
wishes to understand the state of his own convictions
and temper at the time, and to appreciate his unique

[4] " Life of Devonshire ", I, 189.
[5] Gardiner, " Life of Harcourt ", I, 312.

power of moving and inspiring his fellow countrymen, should read the speech which he made in support of them on May 7. It was in some ways the finest effort of his life. It lasted two and a half hours, and was not begun until the dinner hour had been reached, after a long and irritating preliminary wrangle. It ended as follows:

" There is now before the world a glorious prize. A portion of those unhappy people are still, as yet, making an effort to retrieve what they have lost so long, but have not ceased to love and to desire. I speak of those in Bosnia and Herzegovina. Another portion — a band of heroes such as the world has rarely seen — stand on the rocks of Montenegro, and are ready now, as they have ever been during the four hundred years of their exile from their fertile plains, to sweep down from their fastnesses, and meet the Turks, at any odds, for the re-establishment of justice and of peace in those countries. Another portion still, the five millions of Bulgarians, cowed and beaten down to the ground, hardly venturing to look upwards, even to their Father in heaven, have extended their hands to you; they have sent you their petition, they have prayed for your help and protection. They have told you that they do not seek alliance with Russia, or with any foreign Power, but that they seek to be delivered from an intolerable burden of woe and shame. That burden of woe and shame — the greatest that exists on God's earth — is one that we thought united Europe was about to remove; but to removing which, for the present, you seem to have no efficacious means of offering even the smallest practical contribution.

" But, Sir, the removal of that load of woe and shame is a great and noble prize. It is a prize well worth competing for. It is not yet too late to try to win it. I believe there are men in the Cabinet who would try to win it, if they were free to act on their own beliefs and aspirations. It is not yet too late, I say, to become competitors for that prize; but be assured that whether you mean to claim for yourselves even a single leaf in that immortal chaplet of renown, which will be the reward of true labour in that cause, or whether you turn your backs upon that cause and upon your own duty, I believe, for one, that the knell of Turkish tyranny in these provinces has sounded. So far as human eye can judge, it is about to be destroyed. The destruction may not come in the way or by the means that we should choose; but come this boon from what hands it may, it will be a noble boon, and as a noble boon will gladly be accepted by Christendom and the world."

One of the most fastidious and accomplished critics of our time, who was not in sympathy with the views of the speaker, Mr. Balfour, said of this speech twenty years later:

" As a mere feat of physical endurance it was almost unsurpassed; as a feat of Parliamentary courage, Parliamentary skill and Parliamentary eloquence, I believe it will always be unequalled."

Mr. Gladstone's crusade had a strangely disturbing and even distorting effect on the usually cool and dispassionate judgment of the new Lord Beaconsfield.[6] His correspondence with his most intimate friends at this time is full of such expressions as these: —

October, 1876 (to Lord Derby):

Posterity will do justice to that unprincipled maniac Gladstone — extraordinary mixture of envy, vindictiveness, hypocrisy, and superstition; and with one commending characteristic — whether Prime Minister or Leader of Opposition, whether preaching, praying, speechifying or scribbling — never a gentleman.[7]

September, 1877 (to Lady Bradford):

What restlessness! What vanity! And what unhappiness must be his! Easy to say he is mad. It looks like it. My theory about him is unchanged: a ceaseless Tartuffe from the beginning. That sort of man does not get mad at 70. . . . Gladstone, like Richelieu, can't write. Nothing can be more unmusical, more involved or more uncouth than all his scribblement; he has not produced a page which you can put on your library shelves.[8]

January, 1878 (to the same):

I am glad you had time to read Gladstone's speech. What an exposure! The mask has fallen, and instead of a pious Christian we find a vindictive fiend.[9]

---

[6] An earlier illustration of the same kind of lapse is his description of Bright, for whom he had a genuine admiration, on his return to the Gladstone Cabinet in 1873, as that "hysterical old spouter." Buckle, "Disraeli", V, 257.

[7] *Ibid.*, VI, 67.

[8] *Ibid.*, 180–181.

[9] *Ibid.*, 238–239.

It is perhaps only fair, and not wholly irrelevant, to compare the judgment which Mr. Gladstone — some twelve years later — passed on his great rival, in a conversation with Mr. Morley at Biarritz in 1891.

Mr. Gladstone: " For all the deterioration in our public life, one man and one alone, is responsible — Disraeli. He is the grand corrupter. He it was who sowed the seed."

J. Morley: " Ought not Palmerston to bear some share in this? "

Mr. Gladstone: " No, no. Pam had many strong and liberal convictions. On one subject, Dizzy had them too — the Jews. There he was much more than rational — he was practical." [10]

Meanwhile Lord Beaconsfield was not without his own domestic troubles. He writes to the Queen (November, 1877) that in a " Cabinet of twelve members, there are seven parties or policies as to the course which should be pursued ", of which the seventh " is that of Your Majesty, which will be enforced to his utmost by the Prime Minister." The Queen, as her letters show, entered, heart and soul, into this partnership, and when, now and again, in an unwonted fit of prudence, her Prime Minister seemed disposed to give way to his colleagues on this point or that, she rarely failed to supply the necessary stiffening.

This much-divided Cabinet was composed for the most part of mediocrities. The only men in it who

[10] Morley, " Gladstone ", III, 475.

really counted, besides the Prime Minister himself, were Lord Cairns, Lord Salisbury, Lord Derby, and perhaps Sir Stafford Northcote. The breach between Lord Beaconsfield and his oldest and most intimate political friend, Lord Derby, had now become complete. They were working on entirely different lines, which their incompatible temperaments and characters made more and more divergent. In July, 1877, Lord Derby was unfortunate enough to irritate his Sovereign by a letter, in which he stated (what was obviously the truth) that there was " a party which does not conceal its wish for war with Russia. He (Lord Derby) believes that party to be small in numbers, though loud and active. He is quite satisfied that the great bulk of the nation desires nothing so much . . . as the maintenance of peace."

The Queen at once showed the offending document to Lord Beaconsfield (her guest for the moment) who replied in his most soothing vein: " Your Majesty will not deign to notice it, Lord Beaconsfield feels quite sure. Lord Beaconsfield hopes that the great objects of *Your Majesty's imperial policy* may be secured without going to war; but if war is necessary, he will not shrink from advising Your Majesty to declare it, and in that case he very much doubts whether Lord Derby, with all his savage and sullen expressions, will resign."

After many vacillations, Lord Derby however did at last (March, 1878) resign.[11] He was offered the Garter by Lord Beaconsfield, but refused it. His ex-

[11] Lord Carnarvon had preceded him.

planation in the House of Lords of his reasons for retiring from office gave rise to an unseemly speech on the part of his successor, Lord Salisbury, who compared him to Titus Oates. The whole affair is related at length with admirable impartiality by Mr. Buckle in the seventh chapter of his concluding volume. The impression left on the mind of a dispassionate reader is that Lord Derby's is the only figure which comes well out of it.

Lord Beaconsfield reconstructed his Cabinet, giving the Foreign Office to his old enemy, now transformed into a trusted and trustful friend, Lord Salisbury.

CHAPTER VIII

THE controversies of 1877–1879 introduced a new term into our political vocabulary. The expletive "by Jingo" had long been in vogue among the vulgar, and had found its way more than once in the eighteenth century into the pages of writers of the rank and authority of Goldsmith. In 1878 it got into the refrain of a music-hall song, which became for a time the party anthem of the war-mongers; when the British fleet was hovering with the changing moods of a distracted Cabinet, between Besika Bay and Constantinople.

"We don't want to fight, but, by Jingo, if we do,
 We've got the ships, we've got the men, we've got the money too."

Sir Wilfrid Lawson, a strong Gladstonian and a favourite parliamentary wit, took it up, and applied it to the more blustering followers of Lord Beaconsfield, and ever since, "Jingoism" has become the conventional label for a boastful and aggressive patriotism.

Lord Beaconsfield and his new Foreign Secretary, Lord Salisbury, attended the Congress of Berlin, which was held under the presidency of Bismarck in the summer of 1878. The British plenipotentiaries took with them in their pockets two secret Conventions — one between Russia and Great Britain, which provided for the bisection of Bulgaria; the other between Great Britain and Turkey, which sanctioned a British occupation of Cyprus. It was of these transactions — especially of the Turkish Convention — " negotiated in the dark, and ratified in the dark " — that Gladstone used the phrase: " I value our insular position, but I dread the day when we shall be reduced to a moral insularity." The plenipotentiaries brought back from their labours " Peace with Honour " — in other words the Treaty of Berlin, which, as Gladstone freely admitted, had one merit: it liberated eleven millions of people from the Turkish yoke. But in the main it was, as the event showed, a masterpiece of diplomatic shortsightedness and impotence. The two artificially divided Bulgarias were soon reunited; and, before many years more had passed, Austria converted the protectorate which had been given her over Bosnia and Herzegovina into naked annexation. The Cyprus Convention, denounced by Gladstone as an " insane covenant ", was never worth the paper on which it was written.

The Treaty and its authors were, however, received in London and in the House of Commons, with an almost delirious welcome, which intoxicated the Prime Minister, while his more fastidious and phlegmatic colleague detected, behind it all, the artificial activities of the wire-pullers, and grimly predicted that " they would find it out at the polls." [1]

Never was there a shrewder prophecy. In less than two years the whole edifice of Jingoism was shattered into fragments.

In the two years of life which still remained to the Beaconsfield Administration, they were led, sometimes against their judgment, by two " prancing proconsuls " (the phrase is Harcourt's) — Lord Lytton and Sir Bartle Frere — on the Indian frontier and in South Africa, into disastrous adventures which covered them with growing popular discredit.

Lord Lytton, the son of Lord Beaconsfield's old friend, the novelist, and himself a minor poet of some repute, had served his apprenticeship to diplomacy, and was British Minister at Lisbon, when he was selected in 1876, at a most critical moment, to succeed Lord Northbrook in the Viceroyalty of India. The two men first suggested by Mr. Disraeli for the vacant post were Lord Powis and Lord John Manners, two of his associates in the " Young England " movement of the Forties, and the latter his colleague in every Cabinet in which he had sat. Both declined on grounds of health, and Lord Carnarvon, who was next applied to, also refused for domestic reasons. Lord Salisbury, the Secretary of State, was in " despair at the barrenness of the Tory land ", and could only suggest names that seemed to him just " toler-

[1] Lord Salisbury, discussing the subject in conversation two years later said: " I never wish for my foreign policy to be judged by my action in '78. I was only picking up the china that Derby had broken." — " Life of Salisbury ", II, 231–232.

able." [2] The Queen herself mentioned, but only to put it aside, Lord Dufferin, who was a Whig, and then boldly plunged for her *bête noire*, Lord Derby! As Lord Salisbury wrote to his Chief: " The appearance of Derby's name is a charming touch of nature. It reveals a world of untold suffering — and desperate hope." [3] It was then that Lord Beaconsfield turned to Lord Lytton. He was thus the fifth choice.

A year later, when Lytton had started on the " forward " road, and trouble was brewing with Afghanistan, Beaconsfield writes to Salisbury: " We chose him for this very kind of business. Had it been a routine age, we might have made what might be called a more prudent selection, but we foresaw what would occur, and indeed saw what was occurring; and we wanted a man of ambition, imagination, some vanity, and much will — and we have got him." [4]

So the " Forward Policy " was launched.

It was denounced with as much energy by Hartington as by Gladstone himself. It was, he said, " the incarnation and the embodiment of an Indian policy which is everything that an Indian policy should not be."

Gladstone, after dwelling upon the tragic story of the old Afghan War, still living in the minds of the Afghan people, uttered this memorable apostrophe:

" How could they look with friendly eyes upon those who had inflicted those miseries upon them without cause? However, it so happened, that for

[2] Buckle, "Disraeli ", V, 436.   [3] *Ibid.*, V, 437.   [4] *Ibid.*, VI, 379.

the last five and twenty years a succession of wise
and cautious and far-seeing Governments have been
in power both in England and in India, and that every
effort has been made to efface those painful memories. I remember a beautiful description by one of
our modern poets of a great battlefield during the
Punic Wars, in which he observed that for the moment Nature was laid waste and nothing but the
tokens of carnage were left upon the ground; but day
by day and hour by hour she began her kindly task,
and removed one by one, and put out of sight, those
hideous tokens, and restored the scene to order and
to beauty and to peace. It was such a process that
the Viceroys of India had been carrying on for years
in Afghanistan. I now ask — is all this to be undone?
The sword is drawn, and misery is to come upon this
unhappy country again. The struggle may, perhaps,
be short. God grant that it may be short! God grant
that it may not be sharp! "

On the other hand, Lord Beaconsfield at the Lord
Mayor's banquet, 1878, descanted with cynical
serenity, much to the discomfiture of the more prudent of his colleagues, upon the advantages of a
" Scientific Frontier." A little later, in the House of
Lords, he held up his critics to ridicule as advocates
of the " principle of peace at any price " — a doctrine, he added, which had " occasioned more wars
than the most ruthless conquerors. It has dimmed
occasionally for a moment even the Majesty of England. My Lords, you have an opportunity which I
trust you will not lose, and that you will brand these

opinions, these deleterious dogmas, with the repro-
bation of the Peers of England." [5]

The murder of Cavagnari (in May, 1879), the
Resident who had been sent to Kabul under the Treaty
of Gandamak, was avenged by the victorious advance
of Stewart and Roberts, and the occupation of Kandahar. Little more than a year afterwards, when a
Liberal Government came into power, they resolved
to give back Kandahar to Afghanistan. There was,
indeed, no justification, strategic or political, for con-
tinuing to spend a large annual sum, and lock up a
considerable force in a position some three or four
hundred miles from the Indian frontier, and sur-
rounded by a hostile population.[6] The speech of
Lord Hartington in the House of Commons on March
25, 1881, in favour of abandonment, is one of the
most powerful of his parliamentary performances.

A few days earlier in the House of Lords, Lord
Beaconsfield had made the subject his principal topic
in what turned out to be his last public utterance.
After a characteristic gibe at his old colleague, Derby
(" I do not know that there is anything that would
excite enthusiasm in him, except when he contem-
plates the surrender of some national possession "),
he went on to deal in a passage, which has become
historic, with the " Keys of India " :

" There are several places which are called the
Keys of India. There is Merv — then there is a place

[5] December, 1878.
[6] " Life of Devonshire ", I, 313. General Roberts had said in one of
his dispatches, " The less the Afghans see of us the less they will dislike us."

whose name I forget (Herat!); there is Ghuzni, there
is Balkh, there is Kandahar. But, my Lords, the key
of India is not Herat or Kandahar. The key of India
is London. The majesty and sovereignty, the spirit
and vigour of your Parliament, the inexhaustible resources, the ingenuity and determination of your
people — these are the keys of India. But, my Lords,
a wise statesman would be chary in drawing upon
what I may call the arterial sources of his power."

The other pioneer of the Forward Policy, who put
the last nail into the coffin of the Beaconsfield Government, was Sir Bartle Frere, a distinguished Anglo-
Indian of strong character and high-handed methods,
and a convinced adherent of the Forward school.

After the annexation of the Transvaal in 1877 on
the plea that the Republic had fallen into anarchy
and insolvency, and was unable to defend itself
against the Zulus, Frere was sent as High Commissioner by Lord Carnarvon [7] for the ostensible purpose of promoting confederation. He at once got into
trouble with the natives, and without any authority
from the Government at home,[8] sent, in November,
1878, an ultimatum to the most powerful of their
rulers, Cetewayo, the Zulu King, and dispatched a
considerable military expedition to enforce it. The
immediate result was one of the most humiliating

[7] Lord Beaconsfield writes to Lady Bradford (September 27, 1878):
"If anything annoys me more than another, it is our Cape affairs, where
every day brings forward a new blunder of Twitters." This was apparently his familiar nickname for his colleague, Lord Carnarvon; who,
per contra, in private conversation was accustomed to speak of his chief
as "The Jew."

[8] There was in those days no cable to South Africa.

incidents in the annals of our army — the disaster of Isandlana (January, 1879), the shock of which was by no means deadened by the subsequent British victory at Ulundi.

Frere was not recalled (though Beaconsfield expresses in a private letter his own opinion that he " ought to be impeached "); but his wings were clipped when, in spite of the persistent remonstrances of the Queen, Sir Garnet Wolseley (whom the Sovereign disliked, and whom Beaconsfield himself in a letter of August 24, 1879, to her, most unjustly, describes as " an egotist and a braggart; so was Nelson," [9]) was sent out with a commission which gave him plenary authority to handle the Zulu settlement. The whole affair dealt a mortal blow to the prestige of the Government. Their majority in the House of Commons, on a vote of censure proposed by Dilke, fell to sixty.

Meanwhile Mr. Gladstone had been invited to be a candidate, whenever the general election should come, for Midlothian, the premier county in Scotland, and the traditional stronghold of the most powerful of its territorial families. He started his memorable campaign in November, 1879, and the indictment which he preferred against the Beaconsfield régime may be best summarized in his own words: What had been its results?

" Finance in confusion; legislation in arrears, honour compromised by breach of public law; Russia aggrandized and yet estranged; Turkey befriended,

[9] August 24, 1879.

as they say, but sinking every year; Europe restless and disturbed; in Africa the memory of enormous bloodshed in Zululand, and the invasion of a free people in the Transvaal; Afghanistan broken; India thrown back."

A formidable case, in such hands, but Beaconsfield, reassured by one or two misleading by-elections, awaited the issue with unruffled equanimity and indeed, it would seem, with perfect confidence. Rarely even in our chequered electoral history has there been a ruder awakening.

CHAPTER IX

OBSTRUCTION AND THE CAUCUS

THE general election of 1880, with its dramatic reversal of current political values, seemed to the ardent young Liberals of those days — of whom I was one — to open the door to a new era not only of hope but of promise. The next five years, with a few bright interludes, were, on the whole, years of dis-illusionment.

The Parliament which had come to an end had introduced two new factors into our political life: Obstruction and the Caucus — the invention in the main of Parnell and Chamberlain.

Dilatory tactics of a more or less organized kind were of course not unknown in the House of Commons. In 1833, and again in 1843, they had been practised by small groups of members, in both cases against proposals for coercion in Ireland. In the latter year, Lord Palmerston writes: " Experience has shown that a compact body of opponents, though few in number, may by debating every sentence and word of a Bill, and by dividing upon every debate, so obstruct the progress of a Bill through Parliament, that a whole session may be scarcely long enough for carrying through one measure." In the Parliament of

1868 the expedient was amplified and developed on the Conservative side by a group headed by Mr. James Lowther and Mr. G. C. Bentinck, and they were joined (in opposition to Cardwell's military reforms) by a body of reactionary officers, nicknamed the "Colonels."

But it was not till the appearance on the scene of Parnell (1875) that Obstruction became a regular incident of parliamentary procedure. Associated with Biggar and five other Irish members, he showed in the case of the South Africa Confederation Bill of 1877 upon what fragile foundations the whole edifice of parliamentary conventions was built. When the House went into committee on the Bill on July 31, the sitting continued from four o'clock one afternoon till after six on the next. As many as thirteen motions for the adjournment were made, and the minority never rose above five in a division. It is said that on the second day both Lord Beaconsfield and Lord Salisbury paid one of their rare visits to the Peers' Gallery to get a glimpse of the unprecedented scene.

Parnell's object was a purely wrecking one; in his view the first step to Home Rule was to demonstrate that a handful of Irishmen could, at their will, reduce the House of Commons to paralysis and impotence. His methods did not commend themselves to Butt and the bulk of his supporters, but Parnell's following steadily grew. The Radicals under Chamberlain soon took a leaf out of his book, and in 1879 it was due mainly to their persistent obstruction that flogging was abolished in the Army.

The practice was gradually developed into a fine art, and with such deadly effect on legislative efficiency, that it led to drastic changes in parliamentary procedure, the most important of which was the Closure, and what is now known as the Guillotine. Both the older political parties were in turn responsible for tightening up the machine which had got hopelessly out of gear.

The general feeling on the Liberal side is well illustrated by a speech made by Mr. Bright in March, 1882, which was described at the time by perhaps the most expert of the Obstructionists, Mr. Sexton, as showing evidence of " moral retrogression as well as of intellectual decay." " I ask Members whether this House of Commons, with its centuries of service, is to be made prostrate, powerless and useless, at the bidding and by the action of a handful of men who tell you that they despise you, and who, by their conduct, would degrade you. Don't let them suppose that they are greater friends of Ireland than I am. Why, Sir, I acknowledged the wrongs of Ireland, and urged that they should be redressed, when some of those gentlemen opposite were in their long clothes. I am not less the friend of Ireland because I condemn those who, in my opinion, have been of late her worst enemies."

Mr. Gladstone himself was not less emphatic. He described the Irish methods of obstruction as " sometimes rising to the level of mediocrity, and more often grovelling amidst mere trash in unbounded profusion."

But *c'est en forgeant qu'on devient forgeron:* and these crude and, in many cases, unlettered practitioners were the real authors of a permanent revolution in the mechanism of the House of Commons.

Chamberlain was rapidly developing into a considerable Parliamentary figure, often working in close intimacy with Parnell. But the main sphere of his activities in the later Seventies was in the country. He had convinced himself that the revival of Liberalism called for a new machine and a new programme. He was ready to supply both. He started a new organization — the National Liberal Federation, which soon came to be known as the " Caucus ", independent of the central party offices at Westminster, and directly representative of the local associations in the constituencies. It was vehemently denounced by Lord Randolph Churchill, who, however, was astute enough to see its practical conveniences, and adapt it later to his own party. But the " Dragon of Birmingham " (in Harcourt's phrase) was not content with improving the mechanism of the party. He had already set on its legs his policy of Free Schools, Free Land, a Free Church. When the election was over he wrote to Harcourt " indicating the share of the Caucus in the victory ", and adding that " the Liberal lions would demand a solid meal." [1]

[1] Gardiner, " Harcourt ", I, 362.

CHAPTER X

1880

THE House of Commons elected in 1880 was composed of 347 Liberals, 240 Conservatives and 65 Irish Nationalists. The Liberals had thus an ostensible majority of 42 over the other two parties combined.

The election had been fought by the Liberal Party under the nominal leadership of Lord Hartington. At the close of the first Midlothian Campaign (December, 1879) he had written to Lord Granville, announcing his wish to retire, at once and " irrevocably ", in favour of Mr. Gladstone, whom he described as (in the event of a Liberal victory at the polls) the " only possible Prime Minister." Lord Granville strongly demurred to any such step, and was supported by Sir William Harcourt (who still held that there must be " no return from Elba "). He writes to Hartington (December 15, 1879):

" All I can say is that I hope most earnestly you will not flinch from the position you have filled at times when others shrank from the heat and burthen of the day. We have stuck to you, and I hope you will stick to us. For my part my sentiments on this subject are unaltered."

At a conclave of the official Liberal leaders (December 16) it was decided on the advice of the Chief

Whip (Mr. Adam) to make no formal communication for the time being to Mr. Gladstone. It was the
opinion of that astute tactician that, while Mr. Gladstone was in the long run the only possible Prime
Minister, the election should be fought under the
leadership of Lord Hartington. " Those who follow
Mr. Gladstone will all join him in following Hartington, whereas there are many who call themselves
moderate Liberals, but who would not move a finger
to support Mr. Gladstone." [1]

This sagacious advice was adopted, and was, to
all appearance, justified by the result of the election.

The resignation of Lord Beaconsfield; the Queen's
summons to Lord Hartington; the joint advice given
by him and Lord Granville that Mr. Gladstone should
be sent for; and the Queen's ultimate and most
reluctant commission to him to form a government,
accompanied by the warning that he would have to
" bear the consequences " of his previous sayings;
all these things are described with pungent vivacity
in Lord Morley's " Life." It is hardly necessary to
add that Lord Hartington's action throughout was
that of a high-minded and unselfish gentleman.

Strangely enough, the new Cabinet was predomi-
nantly " Whig " in complexion. Six out of its fourteen members were peers. Mr. Gladstone himself was
never, at any time of his life, a Radical,[2] and the only

---

[1] *See* " Life of the Duke of Devonshire ", I, 258–262.

[2] Mr. Holland recalls (" Life of Devonshire ", I, 285) that many
years before a shrewd observer, Archbishop Whately, had described
Gladstone's mind as " full of *culs de sac,* leading to the midst of a
thicket, or the brink of a precipice, without his being aware of it."

avowed Radicals among his new colleagues were the *novus homo* Mr. Chamberlain, and (if they could still be so labelled) Mr. Bright and Mr. Forster. Sir William Harcourt (who had forgotten about Elba) took the Home Office; no label fits him; he stands in a category of his own. Sir Charles Dilke (who was linked by the closest personal and political ties to Chamberlain) was given the most important post outside the Cabinet: the Under-Secretaryship for Foreign Affairs. It is curiously characteristic of Mr. Gladstone that he selected for two important Cabinet offices, in the plethora of fresh ability which was at his disposal, two such men as Mr. Childers and Mr. Dodson. Of the surviving members of the great Cabinet of 1868 Lowe was raised to the peerage; [3] Ripon, who had become a Roman Catholic, was sent as Viceroy to India; and, in some ways the ablest of them, Goschen (who was heretical about the county franchise) accepted the mission of Ambassador Extraordinary to Turkey.

It would not be doing justice to an important side of Mr. Gladstone's complex character to omit the entry in his diary, in which he records his reception, inside and outside, on his first visit to the new House of Commons on May 20, 1880. He was now in his seventy-first year, and was for the second time Prime Minister:

It has not been in my power during these last six months to have made notes, as I would have wished, of my own thoughts and observations from time to

[3] *See ante,* p. 18.

time; of the new access of strength which in some important respects has been administered to me in my old age; and of the remarkable manner in which Holy Scripture has been applied to me for admonition and for comfort. Looking calmly on this course of experience, I do believe that the Almighty has employed me for His purpose in a manner larger or more special than before, and has strengthened me and led me on accordingly, though I must not forget the admirable saying of Hooker, that even ministers of good things are like torches, a light to others, waste and destruction to themselves.[4]

This is couched in a dialect which has ceased to be familiar, but no one who has studied the man, and tried to master the secret of his power, can doubt its sincerity.

[4] Morley, " Gladstone ", III, 1–2.

CHAPTER XI

THE Liberal prospect at the opening of the new
Parliament was to all appearance as nearly unclouded
as any political sky can be. No one who had taken
part in the general election could feel any doubt that
its decisive result was due to a genuine uprising of
popular enthusiasm. The heather had been set on
fire, and the Jingo idol perished in the flames. The
verdict was at once a protest against the policy of
cynicism and adventure which was associated with
the name of Beaconsfield, and of confident hope in
the power and determination of Gladstone to set
things right, and to start with a new and clean departure. I have seen in my time many general elections; some, at which the majority on the winning
side was numerically much more imposing than
in 1880; but I can recall none which was fought by
the rank and file of the victorious host with such
single-minded fervour, or such unwavering and un-
chequered faith.

It is true that Mr. Gladstone was now past
seventy, but no one among his followers doubted
either his physical or his intellectual capacity to
handle the problems of the immediate future. And

among his colleagues on the Treasury Bench, there were at least four — Hartington, Chamberlain, Harcourt, Dilke — any one of whom could be regarded as among his potential successors in the leadership of the party and the first place in the Government. It was, however, none of these tried and famous public performers, but one of the dark horses in the stable, for whom destiny held the prize — if prize it can be called — in reserve. In the obscurity of the lower end of the Treasury Bench, and filling one of the least conspicuous of the minor offices in the Government, no one would have been so surprised or so sceptical as Campbell-Bannerman himself, if he had been told that such was to be his fate.

The official leadership of the Opposition was in the hands of a much more commonplace set of men, with Northcote at the head. It was very soon to become apparent that it was not on that Bench, but below the gangway, that the really formidable assailants of the new Government were to be found. Parnell with his strong and well-disciplined following (some forty out of the sixty Irish Home Rulers) was an incalculable factor that had always to be reckoned with. He had himself given them their general word of command: " We must show these gentlemen " (the British members) " that if they won't do what we want, they shall do nothing else." And the Fourth Party (which never exceeded four in number) became, under Randolph Churchill, the most live and articulate, albeit a wayward and often a mutinous, contingent in the Opposition forces. It was from among its ranks, though not in the person of its brilliant leader, that what would then have seemed the caprice of fortune was to select the future head of the Tory Party. They divided their sarcasms and their sallies pretty impartially between the Liberal Government and their own ostensible Leaders: " the blameless and respectable gentlemen on the front Opposition Bench "; the " bourgeois placemen "; the " Marshalls and Snelgroves "; the " possessors of double-barrelled names so often associated with mediocrity." Gibes and flouts of this order no doubt (as Mr. Disraeli had said years before of Lord Salisbury's invective) " lacked finish ": they shocked the staid rank and file of the Conservative Party; they were rebuked with solemn fatuity by its organs in the Press; but they were relished by the younger and more ardent spirits, who were sadly in need of some " pepper " in their politics; and as their authors were assiduous in their attendance at the House of Commons and almost gluttonous in their parliamentary industry, the Fourth Party soon became something much more formidable than a fitful and audacious adventure.

The steps of the second Gladstone Government were, indeed, doomed from first to last to be dogged by a succession of untoward and intractable situations — some of them wholly unforeseeable; others unexpected in the shape which they actually assumed; and all combining to bring about the indefinite postponement of most of the hopes with which its advent had been hailed.

The first of these misadventures, which almost brought it to its knees in the early days of its first session, was the Bradlaugh episode. It is happily not necessary to rehearse the successive stages of this squalid controversy, which lasted, off and on, for several years. It is enough to say that the new House of Commons did its best to repeat the follies and illegalities of its predecessors in the case of Wilkes. Gladstone took from the first, and throughout, a firm stand on the side of liberty and law; with the result that he was overborne by the majority, and the leadership of the House passed for the moment into the hands of Northcote, spurred on by the Fourth Party, who found here exactly the kind of battle-ground which they would have chosen for the fleshing of their maiden swords.

Bradlaugh retained the confidence of his constituency, by whom he was steadily reëlected; and when, in the next Parliament (1886), he came to the table to be sworn, and the Speaker (Peel) did what his predecessor (Brand) ought to have done in 1880, and refused to permit any intervention against him, the whole thing came to an end with the tacit assent of the Conservatives, who were then, for the moment, in office.

But this discreditable and futile dispute left behind it a permanent addition to the annals of British eloquence, in Gladstone's speech on the second reading of the Affirmation Bill in 1883, which, though he himself modestly described it as " rather Alexandrian ", may be regarded (in Harcourt's words at the time)

as one of the " noblest efforts of human oratory."
The whole of it is well worth the closest study from
students and critics of the art of speaking. The following are perhaps the most moving passages:

Pointing out that the test for admission to membership which had been advocated on the other side was
the test of Theism, he said:

" You draw your line at the point where the abstract denial of God is severed from the abstract
admission of the Deity. My proposition is that the
line thus drawn is worthless, and that much on your
side of the line is as objectionable as the atheism on
the other. If you call upon us to make distinctions,
let them at least be rational. I can understand one
rational distinction, that you should frame the oath
in such a way as to recognize not only the existence
of the Deity, but the providence of the Deity, and
man's responsibility to the Deity; and in such a way
as to indicate the knowledge in a man's own mind
that he must answer to the Deity for what he does,
and is able to do. But is that your present rule?
No, Sir, you know very well that from ancient times
there have been sects and schools that have admitted,
in the abstract, as freely as Christians, the existence
of a Deity, but have held that of practical relations
between Him and man there can be none. Many of
the Members of this House will recollect the majestic
and noble lines:

" Omnis enim per se divom natura necesse est
  Immortali aevo summa cum pace fruatur,
  Semota a nostris rebus sejunctaque longe.

Nam privata dolore omni, privata periclis,
Ipsa suis pollens opibus, nihil indiga nostri,
Nec bene promeritis capitur, nec tangitur ira.

" Divinity exists, according to these, I must say,
magnificent lines, in remote and inaccessible recesses;
but with us it has no dealing, of us it has no need,
with us it has no relation. I do not hesitate to say
that the specific evil, the specific form of irreligion,
with which in the educated society of this country
you have to contend, and with respect to which you
ought to be on your guard, is not blank atheism.
That is a rare opinion very seldom met with; but
what is frequently met with is that form of opinion
which would teach us that, whatever may be beyond
the visible things of this world, whatever there may
be beyond this short span of life, you know, and you
can know, nothing of it, and that it is a bootless
undertaking to attempt to establish relations with it.
That is the mischief of the age, and that mischief you
do not attempt to touch.

" Nay more; you glory in the state of the law that
now prevails. All differences of religion you wish to
tolerate. You wish to allow everybody to enter your
chamber who admits the existence of Deity. You
would seek to admit Voltaire. That is a specimen of
your toleration. But Voltaire was not a taciturn foe
of Christianity. He was the author of that painful
and awful phrase that goes to the heart of every
Christian — and goes, I believe, to the heart of many
a man professing religion who is not a Christian —
écrasez l'infâme. Voltaire was a believer in God; he

would not have had the slightest difficulty in taking the oath. You are working up the country to something like a crusade on this question, endeavouring to strengthen in the minds of the people the false notion that you have got a real test, a real safeguard. And it is for that you are entering on a great religious war. I hold that this contention of our opponents is disparaging to religion; it is idle, and it is also highly irrational. For if you are to have a religious test at all of the kind that you contemplate — the test of Theism — it ought to be a test of a well-ascertained Theism; not a mere abstract idea dwelling in the air, and in the clouds, but a practical recognition of a Divine Governing Power, which will some day call all of us to account for every thought we conceive, and for every word we utter."

These were his concluding words:

" A seat in this House is to the ordinary Englishman in early life, or perhaps, in middle and mature life, when he has reached a position of distinction in his career, the highest prize of his ambition. But if you place between him and that prize not only the necessity of conforming to certain civil conditions, but the adoption of certain religious words, and if these words are not justly measured to the condition of his conscience and of his convictions, you give him an inducement — nay, I do not go too far when I say you offer him a bribe to tamper with those convictions — to do violence to his conscience in order that he may not be stigmatized by being shut out from what is held to be the noblest privilege of the English citizen — that of representing his fellow-citizens in Parliament. And therefore I say that, besides our duty to vindicate the principle of civil and religious liberty, which totally detaches religious controversy from the enjoyment of civil rights, it is most important that the House should consider the moral effect of this test. It is, as Sir H. Drummond Wolff is neither more nor less than right in saying, a purely Theistic test. Viewed as a Theistic test, it embraces no acknowledgment of Providence, of Divine government, of responsibility, or of retribution. It involves nothing but a bare and abstract admission — a form void of all practical meaning and concern. . . . I have no fear of atheism in this House. Truth is the expression of the Divine mind; and however little our feeble vision may be able to discern the means by which God will provide for its preservation, we may leave the matter in His hands, and we may be quite sure that a firm and courageous application of every principle of justice and of equity is the best method we can adopt for the preservation and influence of truth. . . . Great mischief has been done in many minds through a resistance offered to the man elected by the constituency of Northampton, which a portion of the community believe to be unjust. When they see the profession of religion and the interests of religion ostensibly associated with what they are deeply convinced is injustice, they are led to questions about religion itself. Unbelief attracts a sympathy which it would not otherwise enjoy; and the upshot is to impair those convictions and that religious faith, the loss of which I believe to be the most inexpressible calamity which can fall either upon a man or a nation."

Lord Randolph Churchill, with characteristic audacity, attempted a noisy and flimsy reply, which appears to have excited the admiration of his old tutor at Merton, a usually fastidious critic — Doctor Creighton, afterwards Bishop of London. It is a significant indication of the envenomed atmosphere which prevailed, that, despite Mr. Gladstone's appeal, the second reading of the Bill was rejected in a House when the Liberal Party had a nominal majority of nearly fifty over the other parties combined.

It only remains to be added that Bradlaugh became one of the most respected and efficient members of the House, with a strong dash of Conservatism in many of his opinions. In January, 1891, when he lay on his deathbed, the House unanimously expunged from its journals the resolution of 1880 forbidding him to take the oath or make an affirmation. " Does anybody " (asked Mr. Gladstone a few days later) " believe that that controversy so prosecuted and so abandoned, was beneficial to the Christian religion? "

CHAPTER XII

THE TRANSVAAL

MEANWHILE another storm was brewing in a very different quarter. As has already been pointed out, Mr. Gladstone, in the course of his Midlothian campaign, had denounced the annexation of the Transvaal as a stain on the national honour. There can be no doubt that the bulk of his followers expected that, as in the case of Kandahar, which, in spite of an outcry of indignation and obloquy, was handed over to Afghanistan, so also, in South Africa, the Boer Government would be reinstated in the Transvaal. Mr. Gladstone and his colleagues, however, came to the conclusion that such a retrocession would do more harm than good. They were informed that the " great majority of the people of the Transvaal were reconciled to annexation, and that if we reversed the decision of the late Government, there would be a great probability of civil war and anarchy." They accordingly determined to retain the Queen's sovereignty, at the same time promising the Boers, at the earliest opportunity, " the freest and most complete local institutions compatible with the welfare of South Africa."

The Boers rose in arms, and the operations which followed ended in the defeat and death of Sir George

Colley at Majuba Hill. The British Government nevertheless proceeded with the negotiations which had already been initiated before that disastrous incident, and when Lord Roberts, with an overwhelming force, arrived in South Africa, there was no longer any call for military action. The Convention of Pretoria restored the Transvaal Republic, with a reservation of " suzerainty " to the British Crown.

There has rarely been a proceeding which called forth at the moment more violent demonstrations of protest and anger. Ten years later, Lord Randolph Churchill wrote from South Africa, where he was on a visit:

The surrender of the Transvaal, and the peace concluded by Mr. Gladstone with the victors of Majuba Hill, were at the time, and still are, the object of sharp criticism and bitter denunciation from many politicians at home — *quorum pars parva fui.* Better and more precise information, combined with cool reflection, leads me to the conclusion that, had the British Government of that day taken advantage of its strong military position, and annihilated, as it could easily have done, the Boer forces, it would indeed have regained the Transvaal, but it would have lost Cape Colony.

But at the time the taunt that the Government had yielded to force what they had denied to argument was too obvious and too plausible not to be taken advantage of to the full by their critics. Lord Cairns, a great master of what the lawyers call " prejudice ", made the most of the opportunity in a brilliant speech which he delivered in the House of Lords.

" I want to know," he scornfully asked, " what we have been fighting about. If this arrangement was what was intended, why did you not give it at once? Why did you spend the treasure of the country and, still more, why did you shed the blood of the country like water, only to give at the end what you had intended to give at the beginning? " He proceeded, remarking that they were almost worthy of the pencil of a Hogarth, to describe the stages of " The Surrender's Progress." " The Transvaal at this moment," he said, " is the property of the Crown. When the Treaty is carried out the Transvaal will cease to be the property of the Crown. Is not that dismemberment of the Empire? Is not that cession of territory? Is not that abandonment of the Dominions of the Queen?

" I have risen, my Lords, from the perusal of these papers with feelings which I find it difficult to describe. It is not easy, in the midst of the events which pass around us, to realize the character of the history we are creating for future ages, but we can understand and look back upon the history of past times, and infer from this the manner in which we shall be regarded by those who come after us. It is just one hundred years since a page was written in the annals of England, darkened by the surrenders of Burgoyne and Cornwallis. Those were surrenders made by generals at a distance from, and without communication with, home on their own responsibility in great emergency, and without the possibility of any alternative. They were events, however, which both at the time, and long afterwards, deeply touched our national pride. But it will be recorded hereafter that it was reserved for the nineteenth century, and for the days of telegrams, to find a surrender, with reinforcements at hand, and every means for restoring the power and vindicating the authority of the Crown, dictated, word for word, by the Government at home.

" I observe that this arrangement is somewhere styled the Peace of Mount Prospect. My Lords, I much doubt whether it will not go down to posterity as the Capitulation of Downing Street. . . . Other reverses we have had; other disasters. But a reverse is not dishonour, and a disaster does not necessarily imply disgrace. To Her Majesty's Government we owe a sensation which to this country of ours is new, and which certainly is not agreeable.

> " In all the ills we ever bore
> We grieved, we sighed, we wept; we never blushed
> before."

Mr. Chamberlain (who lived to describe the retrocession of the Transvaal as a " disastrous mistake ") was the official apologist in the House of Commons for the ministerial policy. He maintained that as soon as we became acquainted with the true feeling of the Boers, the restoration of their independence was absolutely called for by regard to our former treaty engagements. " A great nation," he said, " could afford to be generous. We had, as a nation, too often proved our courage and tenacity of purpose for any one not blinded by party prejudice to think that our reputation must be made good by pursuing the war to the bitter end. . . . The strength of the giant was there, but it would have been tyrannous to employ it. If the Government had not so employed it, it was because they did not think there was any end to be served commensurate with the sacrifices they would impose upon themselves and others; because they had learned to recognize in their opponents qualities which were worthy of a free people; and, lastly, because they considered that all reasonable demands were satisfied, and that peace gave to this country everything that victory would have enabled them to secure."

The judgment of history upon this transaction will probably accord rather with Lord Randolph Churchill's second thoughts than with Lord Cairns' inflammatory rhetoric. But there can be no doubt that, at the time, the prestige of the Government sustained an ugly wound.

CHAPTER XIII

IRELAND

THE troubles described in the last two chapters were little more than pin pricks in comparison with those which were to come. It was from two such different quarters as Ireland and Egypt that the legislative activity of Parliament in the sphere of domestic reform was all but paralysed, and the vitality of the Government was ultimately drained away.

Lord Beaconsfield, in his letter to the Duke of Marlborough in 1880, had told the country that " a danger in its ultimate results scarcely less disastrous than pestilence and famine distracted Ireland." He called (in phrases that provoked a good deal of ridicule at the time) upon all " men of light and leading " to " consolidate their coöperation " in resisting the new danger threatened by the Home Rule movement to the unity of the Kingdom and the Empire. Mr. Gladstone, in his counter manifesto, dismissed these alarms in a single, almost perfunctory, sentence. And it will be in the memory of those who took an active part in the election and still survive, that Ireland was not in any real sense one of its living issues, but was overshadowed and kept in the background in the great arraignment of the Beaconsfield policy. Mr.

Gladstone himself, some years later, made what he called a " frank admission ":

" I had had much upon my hands connected with the doings of the Beaconsfield Government in almost every quarter of the world, and I did not know the severity of the crisis that was already swelling upon the horizon, and that shortly after rushed upon us like a flood." [1]

Yet a large part of the first session of the 1880 Parliament was taken up with a purely Irish controversy, arising out of a comparatively modest proposal of the Government, to empower the County Courts in certain circumstances to award compensation for disturbance to tenants evicted for nonpayment of rent. The measure was heartily supported by Hartington, and acquiesced in by the other members of the Whig section in the Cabinet, including even the Duke of Argyll. It led, however, to the resignation of Lord Lansdowne (the Under-Secretary for India) and was thrown out in the House of Lords by a majority of more than five to one.

This incident may be regarded as the starting point of the standing quarrel between the Liberal Party and the Upper House, which after thirty years' duration culminated in the passing of the Parliament Act.

It had also the effect of bringing to a head the organization of agrarian disturbance in Ireland. The Land League, created a year before by Michael Davitt, began successfully to defy over a large part of Ireland the Government of the Queen, and at

[1] " Lord Randolph Churchill ", p. 139.

Ennis, in September, 1880, Parnell placed in its hands, and commended to its use, a more effective weapon than the crude and traditional methods of moonlighting, with its violent accompaniments, in the form of boycotting.

The first result was that the Chief Secretary, Forster, by all his convictions and antecedents a Radical and an Anti-Coercionist, who had hitherto resolutely attempted to govern by the ordinary law, felt compelled, with the approval of his colleagues, to bring in as the first Government measure in the session of 1881, a Bill of the utmost stringency, which empowered the detention without trial of persons suspected of treasonable or agrarian offences. In his introductory speech he expressed, with perfect candour, his almost invincible repugnance to embark on such a task. " If I could have foreseen that this would be the result of twenty years of parliamentary life, I would have left Parliament rather than undertake it. But I never was more clear than I am now that it is my duty."

The Bill was to be accompanied by a comprehensive scheme of Land Reform, by which it was hoped to mitigate, and in time altogether to remove, the evils that lay at the root of Irish social disorder. Mr. Bright, the author of the famous apophthegm, " Force is no remedy," who was still a member of the Cabinet, made this abundantly clear. " If," he said, " this Bill were brought in, and if it were not known, and were not promised, that there would be accompanying that Bill, and in the same session of Parliament, a large measure of remedy for the grievances of the Irish people, which are admitted, I should not be sitting on this Bench."

The Coercion Bill occupied twenty-two sittings, which were marked by scenes of obstruction and violence on the part of the Nationalists up to then unprecedented in the House; and it was only by the aid of Speaker Brand's *coup d'état,* the adoption of emergency rules of procedure, and the wholesale suspension of the Irish members, that it was at last got through. Lord Randolph Churchill's final words before it left the Commons were listened to, not without sympathy, by some of Mr. Gladstone's most devoted followers, and in view of the future course of events are well worth recalling:

" This Bill is now passing away from the House, and with it disappears all that liberty-destroying machinery — urgency, *clôtures, coups d'état,* and dictatorships — never, I hope, to return again. We shall now be told to turn our attention to remedial legislation. I make no remark beyond this — that remedial measures which are planted under the shadow of coercion and watered and nourished by the suspension of the Constitution, must be, from their nature, poor and sickly plants of foreign origin, almost foredoomed to perish before they begin to grow. It was upon their capacity to give contentment and happiness to Ireland that the Liberals relied to gain for themselves immortal credit and to secure a perpetual lease of power. The Chief Secretary went to Ireland, bearing with him the hopes and blessings of an enthusiastic and victorious party. He gave us all to understand that he was to become an emancipator greater even than O'Connell; and within twelve months of office he has come to the House to ask for powers more stringent and more oppressive than were ever granted to, or demanded by, Lord Castlereagh, the Duke of Wellington or Lord Grey. I wish the Chief Secretary joy of these beautiful bills; but I may tell the right honourable gentleman that he has acquired by them the undying dislike and distrust of the Irish people. While I have never denied that some measure of this kind, owing to the conduct of the Government, and that alone, was only too necessary for Ireland — and while I have always admitted that, as to the nature and extent of that measure, Her Majesty's Government, who were the culprits, must be the judges — I still recollect, with unqualified satisfaction, that coercion is a double-edged weapon and has before now fatally wounded those Administrators who have been compelled by their own folly to have recourse to it."

The time of the same session (1881) was shared with the prosecution of the twin policy of remedial legislation which was the offset and supplement of coercion. The Irish Land Bill created a Land Court, and gave legislative embodiment to what were called the three F's — Fair Rent, Fixity of Tenure and Free Sale. It was tolerated with sombre acquiescence by Hartington and the Whigs in the Cabinet, with the notable exception of the Duke of Argyll — perhaps Mr. Gladstone's most convinced and fiery sup-

porter through all the stages of the anti-Beaconsfield
campaign. It occupied in its discussions in the House
of Commons fifty-eight sittings, and this part of the
session was appropriately described as the " carriage
of a single measure by a single man." [2] It was, as
has already been pointed out,[3] one of Mr. Gladstone's
most stupendous parliamentary achievements. The
only new reputation to which it gave birth was that
of a hitherto unknown follower of Mr. Parnell, Mr.
T. M. Healy, now Governor of the Irish Free State.
Of the oratory, copious and indeed unmeasured, with
which the debates were enriched, the passage which
best deserves to be rescued from neglect is to be found
in a once famous speech of Mr. Bright.

" To the complaint that the Bill gives so much
to the tenants and takes it all from the landlords, I
should," Bright said, " make this answer. If at this
moment all that has been done by the tenant in Ireland were gone, imagine that! — if all that the
tenants have done were gone, and all that the owners
have done left, — that is the picture, the sort of map
I should very much like to see: It would be charming; it would finish this debate in five minutes, if this
map were drawn; then, over nine tenths of Ireland
the land would be as bare of houses, of barns, of
fences, and of cultivation, as it was in prehistoric
times. It would be as bare as an American prairie
where the Indian now roams, and where the foot of
the white man has never yet trodden."

The Bill was finally carried in the Commons, by

[2] Morley, " Gladstone ", III, 54.   [3] *See ante,* p. 22.

220 to 14, and after some adjustments and compromises was assented to by the House of Lords.

The seesaw policy almost immediately swung to Coercion. Parnell and his associates set deliberately to work to frustrate the operation of the Land Act. Mr. Gladstone, in a famous phrase, declared at Leeds, in October, that the " resources of civilization are not yet exhausted ", and a few days later announced, amidst the enthusiastic plaudits of a Guildhall audience in the City of London, that " the first step had been taken in the arrest of the man who, unhappily, from motives which I do not challenge, which I can not examine, and with which I have nothing to do, has made himself beyond all others, prominent in the attempt to destroy the authority of the law." The machinery of *lettres de cachet,* designed to secure the internment of " village ruffians ", was turned against the leaders of the movement, and Mr. Parnell and some of his principal associates were lodged in Kilmainham Gaol.

His immediate retort was the issue of the " No Rent " manifesto.

Matters steadily went from bad to worse, and agrarian crime continued to increase. Mr. Gladstone, always ready to be taught by experience, resolved on a new departure, and announced in Parliament on May 2, 1882, that the Government intended to introduce a measure for strengthening the ordinary law, and would release the Kilmainham prisoners, and other interned suspects not actually associated with the commission of crime. The Viceroy and the Chief

Secretary wholly disapproved of this reversal of policy and both resigned. Lord Cowper was succeeded by Lord Spencer.

There had been communications between Parnell on the one side and Chamberlain (acting with the assent of Gladstone and the majority of the Cabinet) on the other, which are now of little historical interest, but which gave rise, at the time, to heated controversy over what was called the " Kilmainham Treaty ", one of the terms of which was alleged to be a proffer by Parnell, in exchange for an Arrears Bill, of " cordial coöperation with the Liberal Party."

The assassination in Dublin on May 6, a few days after the " new departure ", of Forster's successor, Lord Frederick Cavendish, and the permanent Under-Secretary, Mr. Burke, opened a new chapter in this dismal and depressing history. Coercion became once more the first order of the day, and by Harcourt's Prevention of Crimes Bill the right to trial by jury was in effect suspended in Ireland. It was supplemented by an Arrears Bill for which the Government received no gratitude. For the next three years the Executive was engaged (not without some measure of success) in Ireland in enforcing the law both against open offenders and secret societies; and in the House of Commons in withstanding an almost daily fusillade of criticism and vituperation from the Nationalist members. Two successive Ministers of very different temperaments — Sir George Trevelyan and Campbell-Bannerman — gallantly bore the brunt of the parliamentary attack, while Lord Spencer, a man of imperturbable courage and serenity, and of sensitive humanity, defied in Dublin the risks of assassination, and pursued, without flinching, the uncongenial task which had been assigned to him.

CHAPTER XIV

EGYPT

THE most tragic chapter in the history of the Second Gladstone Government is to be found in the narrative of its dealings with Egypt; a country the fortunes of which had played even a less conspicuous part than those of Ireland in the controversies which formed the battleground of the general election of 1880.

Here, as in Ireland, the Cabinet were led, step by step, almost unconsciously, certainly without any preconceived or deliberate design, into a policy the very reverse of what might have been predicted either from their antecedents or their predispositions.

A dual financial control had been set up by France and England in the days of the Beaconsfield Administration. The military revolt of 1881, headed by Arabi, with which the weak native Government was unable to cope, brought about widespread anarchy. The intervention of the Turk was vainly invited by the two Western Powers, who sent squadrons to Alexandria in May, 1882. A riot broke out in the town; Europeans were killed; the French fleet withdrew to Port Said; and the bombardment of Alexandria was conducted by the English fleet alone. It was this event which led in the next few years, after an almost incredible series of mischances, to the establishment of a British Protectorate over Egypt and ultimately over the Sudan, with all the contingent risks which such an enormous extension of our responsibilities inevitably entailed.

The immediate result of the bombardment was the resignation of Mr. Bright. Mr. Gladstone's dissuasive letter to him — a masterly presentation of the case for the Government — ends with the statement: " I feel that in being party to this work I have been a labourer in the cause of peace." [1] Mr. Bright, however, thought otherwise. To him a high question of principle was involved, and from his new seat below the gangway in the House of Commons, he gave his view of the matter with the simplicity, the dignity, and the moral elevation, in which he had no rival among the Victorian orators:

" I have no explanation to make; there seems nothing to explain and I have nothing to defend. The simple fact is that I could not agree with my colleagues in the Government in their policy with regard to the Egyptian question.

" For forty years, at least, I have endeavoured from time to time, to teach my countrymen an opinion and doctrine which I hold, namely that the moral law is intended not only for individual life, but for the life and practice of States in their dealings with one another. I think that in the present case there has

[1] It is set out in Morley, " Gladstone ", III, 84–85.

been a manifest violation both of international law
and of the moral law; and therefore it is impossible
for me to give my support to it. I cannot repudiate
what I have preached and taught during the period
of a rather long political life. I cannot turn my back
upon myself and deny all that I have taught to many
thousands of others during the forty years that I
have been permitted at public meetings and in this
House to address my countrymen.

" Only one word more. I asked my calm judgment
and my conscience what was the path I ought to
take. They pointed it out to me, as I think, with an
unerring finger, and I am humbly endeavouring to
follow it."

There followed in rapid succession Wolseley's defeat of Arabi at Tel-el-Kebir, and his deportation
to Ceylon; the occupation of Cairo; and the replace-
ment of dual control by the appointment of an English " agent " and " adviser " in the person of Sir
Evelyn Baring.

There was no intention of permanent occupation
or a complete Protectorate. " The occupation," said
Lord Hartington, " is simply for the purpose of pre-
serving tranquillity in the country, and we trust it
will not be for long." He himself indicated a term of
six months as its probable duration — an estimate
which a few months later Mr. Gladstone (with more
caution) described as " given by way of conjecture
and approximation only."

As late as February, 1885 (after the fall of Khartoum and death of Gordon), Harcourt declared, in the

House of Commons, that he " regarded the permanent occupation of Egypt as the most dangerous policy that could be conceived . . . it would necessitate the annexation of both Egypt and the Sudan." [2]

These and the like declarations, often repeated, were made in perfect sincerity. Towards the end of 1883 instructions were being actually given for the evacuation of Cairo, when the Mahdist rising in the Sudan, and the destruction of an Egyptian force under General Hicks, which had been sent to cope with it without any authority from the British Government, made an immediate retirement from Egypt impossible. But the Cabinet insisted on the abandonment by Egypt of the territory south of Wady Halfa, and the evacuation of the interior of the Sudan. The mission of General Gordon for that purpose, which he converted into an enterprise for " smashing the Mahdi " ; the long delays and vacillations before the expedition for his relief was at last despatched; and the arrival of the advance guard at Khartoum two days after Gordon was killed, are incidents in a melancholy story which was more responsible than any other single cause for the downfall of the Gladstone Government. Their majorities in the House of Commons dwindled almost to vanishing point, and the end which had long been inevitable came, when they were defeated in June, 1885, on an ostensibly unimportant point in the Budget.

[2] Gardiner, "Harcourt", I, 517.

It has been said that the Chapter of Accidents is the Bible of Fools; but there has rarely been in the history of Governments a more conspicuous case of honest intentions irresolutely pursued, and dogged at every step by the malignity of fortune.

CHAPTER XV

AT the end of 1828 Mr. Gladstone, finding the burden of double office too heavy for his strength, gave up the Chancellorship of the Exchequer and chose as his successor Mr. Childers, who was destined to be the immediate agent in bringing about the downfall of the Government. The principal consequential changes were the transfer of Lord Hartington from India to the War Office, and the ascension to the Cabinet as Secretary of State for the Colonies of Lord Derby, who had now definitely broken with his old political associates, and of Sir Charles Dilke, who became head of the Local Government Board and reinforced Chamberlain in the representation of the Extreme Left.

It was from this time that the growing fissure between the two sections of the Cabinet dates its effective origin. The situation was not long afterwards described in a caustic metaphor by Lord Salisbury:

" It is," he said, " rather like one of those Dutch clocks which we used to see in our infancy, where an old woman came out at one time, and an old man came out at another; when the old man came out it

was fine weather, and when the old woman came out
it was the reverse. I would not for a moment attempt
to instance who is the old man or who is the old
woman, but we may safely say that the mechanism
of our political system is this, that when it is going to
be fine weather Lord Hartington appears, and when
Mr. Joseph Chamberlain appears you may look out
for squalls.''

At the celebration of Bright's twenty-five years'
representation of Birmingham in 1883, after advo-
cating a citizen suffrage, with equal electoral districts,
and payment of members, Mr. Chamberlain proceeded to contrast the sober ceremony in which he
was taking part with the pageant of the Russian
Coronation. " The brilliant uniforms," he said, " the
crowds of high officials, the representatives of royalty
were absent, and nobody missed them." It was on
this occasion that he used a phrase which became as
familiar a coin in the currency of contemporary
politics as Mr. Morley's " jingle " about the necessity
of " ending or mending " the House of Lords;[1] he
said:

" Lord Salisbury constitutes himself the spokesman
of a class — of the class to which he himself belongs,
' who toil not, neither do they spin ', whose fortunes,
as in his case, have originated by grants made in
times long gone by, for the services which courtiers
render kings, and which have since grown and in-

---

[1] It seems that a little earlier than this and *à propos* of Ireland Harcourt had told Lord Spencer " not to be alarmed about J. C., who has
a much cooler head than J. Morley." — Gardiner, " Harcourt ", I, 473.

creased while they slept, by levying an unearned share on all that other men have done by toil and labour to add to the general wealth and prosperity of the country of which they form a part."

This speech " led to much correspondence and difficult conversation in high places ",[2] and Gladstone read it with " deep regret ", and when questioned in Parliament, dryly replied that Mr. Chamberlain expressed merely his own opinions. It was followed up by equally uncompromising language at the Cobden Club on June 30, 1883. Mr. Gladstone, writing the next day to his most trusted colleague, Lord Granville, declares that Chamberlain appeared to claim " unlimited liberty of speech " and added that " every extravagance of this kind puts weapons into the hands of opponents, and weakens the authority of Government which is hardly ever too strong and is often too weak already." [3]

Undismayed and impenitent, Chamberlain lost no opportunity during the next two years of developing and pressing the programme in the success of which both his convictions and his ambitions were enlisted. In the midst of the controversy with the House of Lords over the extension of the county franchise and redistribution in 1884–1885, he was fully alive to the importance, from the point of view of influencing the new electorate, of emphasizing the social side of prospective new departures in Liberal policy. It was in this sense that he declared at Ipswich (January, 1885) that this country had been " called the para-

[2] Morley, " Gladstone ", III, 112.   [3] *Ibid.*, III, 113–114.

dise of the rich ", and warned his hearers " no longer to allow it to be the purgatory of the poor."

In the early part of 1885 while he was still a Minister, he asked on one platform: " What ransom will property pay for the security it enjoys? " and declared on another that " if the rights of property are sacred, surely the rights of the poor are entitled to an especial reverence; Naboth's vineyard [4] deserves protection quite as much as Ahab's palace."

These and the like phrases aroused much uneasiness at Windsor, from which quarter Mr. Gladstone was the recipient of sharp remonstrances.

Mr. Chamberlain's social programme, most of which has since been carried into law at the instance of one or other of the old parties, was regarded at the time with consternation by the Tories, and with scarcely concealed aversion by Lord Hartington and the Whig section of his colleagues. Mr. Gladstone's own attitude towards it was never clearly defined. Perhaps the nearest approach to an illuminating glimpse into the real state of his mind is to be found in a letter [5] which he wrote to Lord Hartington in the autumn of 1885 (November 10) on the eve of the then impending general election:

I wish to say something (in his election speeches) about the modern Radicalism. But I must include this, that, if it is rampant and ambitious, the two most prominent causes of its forwardness have been —

[4] Naboth, it would seem from the scriptural record, belonged to the class of hereditary landowners. *See* I Kings, xxi.

[5] " Life of Devonshire," II, 91.

1. Tory democracy.

2. The gradual disintegration of the Liberal aristocracy. . . .

I am sorry that Chamberlain raises and presses his notion about the compulsory powers for the local authorities. I should have said, try freedom first. But when it is considered how such a scheme must be tied up with safeguards, and how powerful are the natural checks, I hardly see, and I am not sure that you see, in this proposal *stuff* enough to cause a breach.

I am no partisan in fine of Chamberlainism, but I think some " moderate Liberals " have done much to foster it; and that if we are men of sense, the crisis will not be yet.

Strangely enough, the real rifts in the Cabinet, which brought about its ultimate disintegration in 1885, had little or nothing to do with the Chamberlain programme. They were concerned almost entirely with the latest phases in the development of the Egyptian and still more of the Irish problem. The most vivid account of them is to be found in the almost daily extracts from the Journal kept for Sir William Harcourt by his son, which are set out in Mr. Gardiner's " Life of Harcourt." [6]

The two questions to be settled in regard to Ireland were (1) the renewal, and in what shape, and for what time, of coercion, and (2) the choice between confining the reform of local government to the setting up of representative County Boards, and of supplementing them with a Central Board (of strictly

[6] Vol. I., pp. 524 *et seq.*

limited powers) for Ireland as a whole. The latter question arose at the close of a Cabinet (after Sir W. Harcourt had left) on May 9, 1885. The Central Board plan, which was fathered by Mr. Chamberlain and known to have, at any rate, the provisional approval of Mr. Parnell, was opposed by all the peers in the Cabinet except Lord Granville, and supported by all the commoners except Lord Hartington. It was, therefore, put aside. When the Cabinet rose, Mr. Gladstone said to Mr. Chamberlain: " Did you ever see such men? If God spares them for three years, they will be on their knees repenting that they have not agreed to this." [7] He wrote to the Viceroy, Lord Spencer, that Chamberlain's " scheme was dead for the present only. It will quickly rise again, as I think, perhaps in larger dimensions." [8]

The state of Cabinet chaos which at once developed is depicted in the Harcourt Journal:

May 15. Cabinet to-day. Spencer had intended to produce a Land Purchase Bill for Ireland this session, but at the Cabinet, Chamberlain and Dilke said they would not have it without the Central Council, as their scheme had been that the Council should deal with this question . . . So Chamberlain and Dilke resigned. W. V. H., with great difficulty induced them to stay, and then Spencer resigned, saying that all his schemes for the government of Ireland had been destroyed, and he had been thrown over by his colleagues. Ultimately W. V. H. induced him to withdraw his resignation; and Gladstone made

[7] Gardiner, " Harcourt ", I, 525; comp. Morley, " Gladstone ", III, 194.

[8] Morley, *ibid.*

a confused and confusing statement about the Crimes
Bill in the House, which made nothing clear except
that the Coercion Bill would not be accompanied by
any remedial legislation.

May 16. Another Cabinet to-day. Childers has
resigned.

On May 19 Harcourt wrote to Spencer:

Things are no better here. The Cabinet seems like
a man afflicted with epilepsy, and one fit succeeds
another, each worse than the last. We had Childers
down on Saturday moribund, and he was with difficulty picked up, but swears he will die, and no one
shall save him from perishing with the Budget after
Whitsuntide. Poor Gladstone seems worn out — and
no wonder. Everyone wishes to go at once. But how
and why and on what pretext? The Party in the
country and the House of Commons are united
enough, and only anxious to support a Government
which is resolved on suicide.

The Journal continues:

May 20. W. V. H. has had a hard day's work at
the House of Commons negotiating with Chamberlain, Dilke and Gladstone. He told the latter (who
had privately informed Harcourt ten days before
that " he had finally made up his mind to resign " [9])
" that if he could have a promise from him that he
would remain Prime Minister till the end of the
Session, he thought he could arrange matters " G.
gave him this pledge, and W. V. H. then saw Chamberlain and Dilke, and told them that if Gladstone
was prepared to carry this Budget through, he (W.

[9] Gardiner, " Harcourt ", I, p. 524.

V. H.) could not quarrel with him on a question of finance, much as he disliked the proposals. Dilke said if that was so he must also give way, as his resignation would necessarily take with it Chamberlain, who does not really care much about the Budget question one way or the other.

Through some extraordinary misunderstanding of the real position of Chamberlain and Dilke, Mr. Gladstone on this same day (May 20) announced in the House of Commons that the Government had determined to introduce a Land Purchase Bill. This made confusion worse confounded. " Chamberlain," according to the Journal, " returned to W. V. H.'s room in a furious rage, saying that he had been vilely tricked by Gladstone." Chamberlain and Dilke at once sent in their resignations, but agreed, after some attempts to patch up the misunderstanding, to keep them in suspense. Harcourt's own view was that they were " glad to have an opportunity to upset the coach." [10]

The situation on the eve of the Whitsuntide recess is thus summed up in the Journal:

Each section of the Cabinet thinks that it has been betrayed on one subject or another by Gladstone: Chamberlain and Dilke say they have been tricked over the Land Purchase Bill; Childers thinks he has been betrayed over his Budget; Spencer thinks he has been abandoned on the Crimes Bill; and Northbrooke and Selborne believe they have been deceived on the Sudan policy.

Harcourt, the worn-out peacemaker, went to sea

[10] Gardiner, " Harcourt ", I, p. 528.

for Whitsuntide, and while " dodging about the Channel " in the steam yacht, *Zingara,* wrote to Spencer, washing his hands of the whole business. Mr. Gladstone retreated to Hawarden, where he " dived into Lechler's ' Wycliffe ', Walpole's ' George III ', Conrad on German Union, and Cooper on the Atonement ",[11] and notes in his diary that, on his return to London, he read " Amiel's Journal " and Edersheim on the Old Testament, and went twice to the Chapel Royal on Trinity Sunday.

The final blow came from what was to the outside world a wholly unexpected quarter.

The Harcourt Journal records that on June 5 the Cabinet made some slight changes in the Budget:

Whereupon Childers jumped up, saying, " I cannot stand this " and left the room. W. V. H. . . . followed him to his room in the Treasury, where he was walking up and down in a state of great excitement. They were presently joined by Gladstone, and W. V. H. and Gladstone walked up and down the room on each side of Childers, until he said he would take an hour to reconsider his position. They left him alone and then sent up Granville and Selborne, who, it is supposed, prayed with and over him. Ultimately he promised not to resign." [12]

Three days later the Government were defeated by a majority of twelve on an amendment to the Budget proposed by Sir Michael Hicks Beach, and supported by a combination of Tories, Parnellites and

[11] Morley, " Gladstone ", III, 196.
[12] Gardiner, " Harcourt ", I, p. 526.

the Fourth Party. A large number of Liberals (74) abstained from voting.

" This," remarks Mr. Gladstone, in a concise entry in his diary, " is a considerable event."

It was in fact the end of the Second Gladstone Administration.

CHAPTER XVI

TORY RIFTS: THE RISE OF CHURCHILL

REFERENCE has already been made (Chapter XI) to the emergence of the Fourth Party in the session of 1880 as a new and separate parliamentary factor, and to its successful début in the discreditable manœuvres to exclude Mr. Bradlaugh from the House of Commons. The new party had, in the background, the sympathy of no less a personage than Lord Beaconsfield. During the autumn of 1880 he invited Mr. Gorst, with whom in the old days of party re-organization he had been on intimate terms, to visit him at Hughenden. " Lord Beaconsfield," wrote Mr. Gorst to his associates, " was in his talk anything but Goaty; [1] he generally expressed great confidence in us, thought we had a brilliant future before us, and promised to help and advise us as much as he could." [2] He recommended them, however, to stick to North-cote. In a conversation with Sir Henry Wolff of about the same date, he spoke in the same sense: " He (Northcote) represents the respectability of the party. I wholly sympathize with you all, because I never was respectable myself. In my time the re-

[1] " The Goat " was the derisory epithet which the Fourth Party were accustomed to apply to their nominal leader, Sir S. Northcote.
[2] " Lord Randolph Churchill ", p. 126.

spectability of the party was represented by . . . , a horrid man; but I had to do as well as I could; you must do the same. Don't on any account break with Northcote but defer to him as often as you can. Whenever it becomes too difficult you can come to me, and I will try to arrange matters." [3] Whether to acquire a flavour of respectability, or to flout Sir Stafford, a public meeting was arranged to be held at Woodstock, where, on November 30, 1880 (as Mr. Winston Churchill tells us), " under a temporary roof of tarpaulins, Lord Salisbury and Lord Randolph Churchill first appeared together in political association." [4]

Lord Beaconsfield's death in the spring of 1881 opened up the question of the leadership of the Tory Party. The choice lay between Lord Salisbury and Sir Stafford Northcote. There seems to be little doubt that then, and for some time afterwards, the great bulk of the Conservatives in Parliament would have approved the selection of Northcote, whom they regarded as a safe man, in preference to Lord Salisbury, whom they feared as dangerous and erratic. The Fourth Party itself was acutely divided on the personal question. When Lord Beaconsfield's statue came to be unveiled on the anniversary of his death in April, 1883, the principal part in the ceremony was assigned to Sir Stafford, and to Lord Salisbury was relegated the subsidiary task of moving a vote of thanks to his rival. Lord Randolph at once jumped into the fray as an ardent pro-Salisbury champion,

[3] " Lord Randolph Churchill ", pp. 127–128.   [4] *Ibid.*, p. 130.

and in letters to the *Times*, and a magazine article entitled " Elijah's Mantle ", he wrote as many disagreeable and disparaging things as a caustic and undisciplined pen could devise about Sir Stafford, and the " old gang " who occupied the Front Opposition Bench in the Commons. Amid the storm which his outburst aroused among the " respectabilities " of the party, he declared that he was " only too happy to be the scapegoat on which doomed mediocrities may lay the burden of their exposed incapacity." [5]

The immediate result was the formation of the Primrose League, called after a homely woodland plant, which for some unexplained reason was believed to be Lord Beaconsfield's favourite flower, though almost the only mention of it in his works is said to be as a desirable ingredient in a salad. The idea originated in the fertile brain of Sir Henry Wolff. It was at once taken up by Lord Randolph; it formed a new bond of union for the disintegrated Fourth Party; and though (as Mr. Churchill says) " in its beginnings viewed with sour distrust by all Conservatives who were officially orthodox, virtuous, and loyal ", it inflamed the imagination of the rank and file, and starting with less than a thousand members, the new organization claimed after twenty-one years of life to have 1,700,000 Knights, Dames and Associates on its rolls. It was unquestionably in its day a useful instrument of Tory propaganda, and an effective auxiliary to the official party machine.

[5] " Churchill ", p. 200.

Photograph by Russell of London

LORD RANDOLPH CHURCHILL

The problem of leadership was for the moment shelved. But there have been few more curious personal phenomena in British politics than the rapid rise during these years of Lord Randolph Churchill to a position of something very like ascendancy with the rank and file of the Tory Party in the constituencies. He was caricatured, derided, nicknamed; but, as his son truly says, he had become, in 1883, " unquestionably the most popular speaker " at Conservative meetings in the country. He had extraordinary natural gifts of speech which were cultivated with the most assiduous care; his industry was tireless, and his audacity unfailing; he was insensitive to criticism and to ridicule; he was totally free from the restraints of good taste; and he possessed, perhaps in a greater degree than any of his contemporaries, all the arts and the artifices of the demagogue. In private he could be one of the most charming of companions, and, as I can testify with a grateful memory, lavish of kindness and encouragement to men younger and less experienced than himself, in every quarter of politics. His faults were largely those of temperament, but he was fatally lacking in the sovereign quality of judgment. Whether he would ever have matured into a real statesman, or even an endurable colleague, is an unsolved problem. He twice held high posts — at the India Office and the Exchequer. His term of office was in each case too brief to provide a trustworthy test of his capacity, though in both departments he left upon the minds of the eminent officials who worked under him and were, to say the least, not predisposed in his favour, the impression of an efficient and resourceful chief.

Of his speeches during this phase of his career, the severest critic must acknowledge that they are at any rate eminently readable. Perhaps the most characteristic specimen is one which he made at Blackpool in the early part of 1884, in which he singled out Mr. Chamberlain and Mr. Gladstone as the targets for his invective. One or two passages may be selected for the benefit of readers who are innocent enough to think, comparing the past with the present, that there was something dull and decorous in the polemics of the Victorian Age.

His first victim was Mr. Chamberlain, *à propos* of the attack on those who " neither toil nor spin " :

Just look at what Mr. Chamberlain himself does. He goes to Newcastle and is entertained at a banquet there, and procures for the president of the feast a live Earl — no less a person than the Earl of Durham. Now Lord Durham is a young gentleman who has just come of age, who is in the possession of immense hereditary estates, who is well known on Newmarket Heath, and prominent among the gilded youth who throng the corridors of the Gaiety Theatre, but who has studied politics about as much as Barnum's new white elephant. If by any means it could be legitimate, and I hold that it is illegitimate, to stigmatize any individual as enjoying great riches for which he has neither toiled nor spun, such a case would be the case of the Earl of Durham; and yet it is under the patronage of the Earl of Durham, and basking in the smiles of the Earl of Durham, bandying vulgar compliments with the Earl of Durham,

that this stern patriot, this rigid moralist, this un-
bending censor, the Rt. Hon. Joseph Chamberlain,
flaunts his radical and levelling doctrines before the
astounded democrats of Newcastle.

This is a pretty bad descent, not only from the
finished efforts of a great master of invective like
Disraeli, but from the worst excesses of Junius or
even of Cobbett. A still deeper note of vulgarity is
struck in the attack which follows upon Mr. Gladstone:

The Prime Minister is the greatest living master
of the art of personal political advertisement. Hollo-
way, Colman, and Horniman are nothing compared
with him. Every act of his, whether it be for the purpose of health or of recreation or of religious devotion, is spread before the eyes of every man, woman
and child in the United Kingdom on large and glar-
ing placards. For the purposes of an autumn holiday
a large transatlantic steamer is specially engaged, the
Poet Laureate adorns the suite, and receives a peerage as his reward, and the incidents of the voyage are
luncheon with the Emperor of Russia and tea with
the Queen of Denmark. For the purposes of recreation he has selected the felling of trees. . . . Every
afternoon the whole world is invited to assist at the
crashing fall of some beech or elm or oak. The forest
laments in order that Mr. Gladstone may perspire,
and full accounts of these proceedings are forwarded
by special correspondents to every daily paper every
recurring morning. For the purposes of religious devotion the advertisements grow larger. The parish
Church of Hawarden is insufficient to contain the
thronging multitudes of fly-catchers who flock to hear

Mr. Gladstone read the lessons for the day, and the humble parishioners are banished to hospitable Nonconformist tabernacles in order that mankind may be present at the Prime Minister's rendering of Isaiah or Jeremiah, or the Book of Job.[6]

It might have been supposed that this mud-slinging — despite occasional flashes of wit and felicities of phrase — directed against the most venerable and illustrious figure in British or indeed European politics, would have excited universal nausea. But Lord Randolph had taken a different measure of the taste of the " Tory Democracy ", which he conceived it to be his mission first to " educate ", and ultimately to lead.

[6] " Churchill ", pp. 228–229.

CHAPTER XVII

CHURCHILL, 1883–1885

IN the spring of 1884 Lord Randolph Churchill announced his intention to enter the electoral lists in Birmingham and attack the stronghold of Mr. Bright and Mr. Chamberlain. As usual, he did not mince his words: " The robe of righteousness " (he declared, at Woodstock) " with which he (Mr. Bright) and his confederates have clothed their squalid and corrupted forms shall be torn asunder . . . and all shall be disclosed which can be, whether it be the impostor and the so-called ' people's tribune ', or the grinding monopolies of Mr. Chamberlain, or the dark and evil deeds of Mr. Schnadhorst." [1]

It is remarkable that, in contrast with Mr. Chamberlain, who was already expounding and propagating his " unauthorized programme ", Lord Randolph and his friends were admittedly at this time without any constructive policy of their own. He coquetted, it is true, for a moment with " Fair Trade " — the then current *alias* for Protection — and in his speech at Blackpool he announced the notable discovery that " turn your eyes where you will, survey any branch of British industry you like, you will find signs of

---

[1] " Churchill ", p. 232.

mortal disease. . . . What has produced this state of things? Free imports? I am not sure: I should like an inquiry; but I suspect free imports of the murder of our industries, much in the same way as if I found a man standing over a corpse and plunging his knife into it, I should suspect that man of homicide." [2]

In opening his candidature at Birmingham, with a characteristic stab at the " old gang ", he acknowledged that his party were bankrupt of any definable policy. " I do not know what will be the policy of the Tory Party. I am not the least bit in the confidence of the leaders. . . . I have not been able to gather from their speeches or their acts what would be the policy they would adopt if the responsibility of government was placed upon them." And then he proceeded to this singularly impotent conclusion: " I think I can tell you what their policy ought to be. . . . what I will try and make it to be. . . . It shall be a policy of honesty and courage. It shall be a policy which will grapple with difficulties and not avoid them or postpone them. It shall be a popular policy and not a class policy. It shall be a policy of activity for the national welfare, combined with a zeal for Imperial security." [3]

The " hungry sheep " of the Tory democracy were left to digest, with such relish as they could command, these unappetizing platitudes.

Perhaps the nearest approach to a formula is to

[2] " Churchill ", p. 237. It is only fair to record that he seems soon to have recovered from this passing aberration.
[3] *Ibid.*, p. 235.

be found, again in his Blackpool speech, where, after
reviling the Whigs as a " Class " and the Radicals as
a " Sect ", he declares the Tory Party to be the only
safe custodians of our ancient institutions — democratic, aristocratic, parliamentary, monarchical —
" uniting in an indissoluble embrace religious liberty
and social order — the inspired offspring of Time."

" And now for our cry," said Mr. Taper.[4] " Ancient
institutions and modern improvements, I suppose,
Mr. Tadpole?":[1] those " glorious institutions " under
which (according to Coningsby, Mr. Disraeli's typical
" Young England " hero) " the Crown has become a
cipher; the Church a sect; the Nobility drones; and
the People drudges." [5]

Even Mr. Winston Churchill's literary art cannot
make interesting the necessarily tedious details of the
long tussle between Lord Randolph and the " Goats "
for the control of the Tory Party machine. After
a protracted series of " intrigues and counter-in-
trigues ", and, finally, the feverish activities of " all
sorts of busybodies who ran to and fro like shuttles
weaving up a piece ", the contest ended for the
moment in a substantial triumph for the malcon-
tents, and Lord Randolph, " neither disarmed nor
placated ", was seated firmly in the chair of the Conservative Caucus.[6]

[4] " Coningsby ", Book II, Chapter VI.
[5] *Ibid.*, Book V, Chapter II.
[6] " Churchill ", pp. 267–268.

The quarrel was finally patched up in the summer and autumn of 1884, largely through the activities of Sir Michael Hicks Beach, a capable and ambitious man, with a temper which was perhaps one of his most valuable political assets, and an assertive personality which was wanting (notwithstanding superior intellectual powers) in Sir Stafford Northcote. Northcote himself was at last induced to speak (October, 1884), with and for Lord Randolph, at a gigantic demonstration organized with infinite care at Aston Park in the neighbourhood of Birmingham. The Radicals of Birmingham, resenting this intrusion into the purlieus of their holy ground, got up a counter-demonstration on a considerable scale to be held on a vacant plot of land hard by the park wall. It was alleged that they also obtained admission (partly by means of forged tickets) in large numbers into the Tory meeting. The result was a mêlée which soon developed into a formidable riot, and both Sir Stafford and Lord Randolph were, with difficulty, carried out of the danger zone by their friends.

A vivid description of this incident, and of the parliamentary controversies to which it led, is to be found in Mr. Churchill's " Life " of his father. Meanwhile, Sir M. Hicks Beach had with general consent succeeded Lord Randolph in the chair of the Caucus. In Mr. Churchill's words, he laid the National Union to rest (for nearly twenty years) " in an obscurity from which its members only emerged at infrequent intervals to pass Protectionist resolutions." [7] The rifts in the Tory organization had, so far as the rank and file were concerned, been closed. But, as will be seen in the immediate sequel, personal questions of vital import to the future of the party still remained to be solved.

[7] " Churchill ", p. 291.

CHAPTER XVIII

REFORM

THE great legislative achievements of the 1880 Parliament, apart from the Irish Land Bill, were the Acts for the extension of the County Franchise, and for a Redistribution of Seats, which became law in its last two sessions.

The Franchise Bill, which was first introduced in 1884, was not seriously opposed on its merits. The second reading was carried in the Commons by a majority of 130, and the third reading without a division. The main point of contention in Committee was the inclusion of Ireland, upon which, however, the Opposition were by no means united. The most effective protest was that made by David Plunket, one of the Irish minority, who, though afflicted by an impediment in his speech, was generally regarded in the House as (after Gladstone and Bright) its most finished orator. He predicted, in sombre and impressive tones that the extension of the Bill to Ireland would prove to be the first step towards the repeal of the Union.

The favourite argument with the Tory rank and file was that which was put forward by Mr. W. H. Smith, an eminent representative of the new Con-

servative bourgeoisie, who had been singled out by
Mr. Disraeli for a place in his Cabinet. He was
totally without any pretence to oratorical gifts, but
he had the reputation of being an excellent man of
business, and his geniality and good temper made him
universally popular in the House of Commons, of
which, by an incalculable freak of destiny, he was
later to become the leader. According to Mr. Smith,
no votes could safely be given to Irish peasants who
lived in mud cabins. The " mud-cabin argument "
(as it was called) was made the most of in the debate, until it was finally demolished by Lord Randolph
Churchill, in one of his most effective Parliamentary
sallies:

" I suppose that in the minds of the lords of subur-
ban villas, of the owners of vineries and pineries, the
mud cabin represents the climax of physical and
social degradation. But the franchise in England has
never been determined by Parliament with respect to
the character of the dwellings. The difference between the cabin of the Irish peasant and the cottage
of the English agricultural labourer is not so great as
that which exists between the abode of the right
honourable member for Westminster and the humble
roof which shelters from the storm the individual
who now has the honour to address the Committee.

> " Non ebur neque aureum
> Mea renidet in domo lacunar:
> Non trabes Hymettiae
> Premunt columnas ultima recisas
> Africa."

It may be remarked, as one of the many changes which have taken place in our time in parliamentary conventions, that it would be difficult to imagine a member (however distinguished) venturing to-day to quote five lines of Horace in a debate in Committee. It was still assumed, forty years ago, that the text of the great Latin authors was familiar to the bulk of members; and (as we have seen) in his unrivalled speech on the Affirmation Bill, Mr. Gladstone declaimed a passage of six lines from Lucretius.[1]

The House of Lords threw out the Franchise Bill on the ground that it was not accompanied by any adequate security that Redistribution would be effected at the same time.

There ensued a violent agitation in the country, in which the most conspicuous voice was that of Mr. Chamberlain, whose denunciations of the Second Chamber reached a climax in his speech at Denbigh (October 20, 1884). " The chronicles of the House of Lords " (he declared) " are one long record of concessions delayed until they have lost their grace, of rights denied until extorted from their fears. . . . *The cup is nearly full.* The career of high-handed wrong is coming to an end. . . . We have been too long a Peer-ridden nation, and I hope you will say to them that, if they will not bow to the mandate of the people, they shall lose for ever the authority which they have so long abused."

The controversy was, however, settled by a com-

[1] I have dealt more at length with the change of fashion in a later chapter.

Photograph by Russell of London

W. H. SMITH

promise. The Queen intervened, and at her suggestion negotiations were begun between the party
leaders. After many ups and downs, Mr. Gladstone,
Lord Salisbury, and Sir S. Northcote sat together
round a tea table at Number 10, Downing Street, and
by the end of November Mr. Gladstone was able to
inform the Queen " that ' the delicate and novel communications ' between the two sets of leaders had
been brought to a happy termination." [2]

The extended franchise was passed into law, the
principles and machinery of the new distribution of
areas having been previously embodied in a bill
which received legislative assent in the session of
1885. No one in any party foresaw that the new
reform would be followed, with a brief interregnum
in 1892–1895, by nearly twenty years of Tory Government.

A record of what, in spite of the manifold distractions and mischances described in the last few
chapters, was actually accomplished by the second
Gladstone Government was given later by Mr. Chamberlain. (Birmingham — June 3, 1885.)

" We have abolished flogging in the Army; we
have suspended the operation of the odious Acts
called the Contagious Diseases Acts; we have
amended the game laws; we have reformed the burial
laws; we have introduced and carried an Employers'
Liability Bill; we have had a Bankruptcy Act, a
Patents Act and a host of secondary measures, which
together would have formed the stock-in-trade of a

[2] Morley, " Gladstone ", III, 138.

Tory Government for twenty years at least. And these are the fringes only, the outside of the more important legislation of our time, the chief elements in which have been the Irish Land Bill and the Reform Bill."

CHAPTER XIX

THE ADVENT OF THE CARETAKERS

THE actual downfall of the Gladstone Government was occasioned, as has been pointed out, by the carrying, in a comparatively thin House, by a small majority, of a by no means vital amendment to the Budget. It is described by Mr. Churchill,[1] as having been " artfully and deliberately contrived to unite the Opposition on an issue " (the beer duty) " easily defensible in the country, and likely to secure support from the Irish, and from the liquor interest in the House." But there can be little doubt that, notwithstanding the intestine distractions already described, which were making havoc of Cabinet unity, Mr. Gladstone could the next day have obtained from the House of Commons a substantial majority for a vote of confidence. He determined, however, to the surprise of the Sovereign, of his own party, and probably of the Tory Party also, on immediate resignation.

The decisive factor in the division had been, of course, the Parnellite vote, which was given, it need hardly be said, with little, if any, regard to the actual merits of the case. The liquor interest, though it was powerfully represented among the rank and file of

[1] " Lord Randolph Churchill ", p. 323.

the Nationalists, was in no sense a dominating factor, and, if Mr. Parnell had so willed, the party as a whole would (according as he directed) have abstained, or even voted with the Government.

The real truth is that the Nationalists, who had, or imagined that they had, a long score to settle with the Government, knew that the Cabinet were in two minds as to the renewal of the Crimes Act. If they could have anything in the nature of an assurance, or even a reasonable expectation, that a Conservative Administration would drop the Act, they were ready to do all that they could to put such an Administration in power. It would seem that Mr. Gibson (afterwards Lord Ashbourne) who was the principal adviser of the Tory Opposition on Irish matters (he used to be called by Lord Randolph " The Family Solicitor ") had managed to persuade himself, and, at any rate, to half-persuade a majority of his colleagues, that for the moment Ireland could be governed without coercion. But a large majority of the rank and file of the party had not yet been educated to that point of view, and an actual and avowed bargain between the official leaders and Mr. Parnell would have been far too risky a proceeding. Lord Randolph, however, did not feel himself in any way precluded from entering into " conversations " on the subject with the Irish leader, and was perfectly frank as to his own position. " I told Parnell " (he said, a year later, to Lord Justice Fitzgibbon) " when he sat on that sofa, that if the Tories took office and I was a member of their Government, I would not

consent to renew the Crimes Act." This seems to
have been good enough for Parnell, who replied, " In
that case you will have the Irish vote at the elections." [2]

The question of the future Tory leadership was
finally decided by the action of the Queen in sending
for Lord Salisbury. A dissolution was for the time
impossible in consequence of the still unsettled state
of the new registers. Lord Salisbury was genuinely
disinclined to undertake the task of forming a Government, but was persuaded by the Queen to make
the attempt if Mr. Gladstone persisted (as he did)
in refusing to resume office. Meanwhile the Queen
offered Mr. Gladstone an Earldom, an offer which he
gratefully declined in a letter set out in full in Lord
Morley's " Life." [3] One characteristic passage may
be quoted:

> Any service that he (Mr. G.) can render, if small,
> will, however, be greater in the House of Commons
> than in the House of Lords; and it has never formed
> part of his views to enter that historic chamber, al-
> though he does not share the feeling which led Sir
> R. Peel to put upon record what seemed a perpetual,
> or almost a perpetual, self-denying ordinance for his
> family.

Lord Salisbury proceeded with the ungrateful task
of constructing what Mr. Chamberlain described as
his " Ministry of Caretakers ", and at the outset he
had to encounter a most formidable difficulty. He

[2] " Churchill ", p. 320.
[3] " Gladstone ", III, 209.

had naturally assigned the office of Chancellor of the Exchequer and Leader of the House of Commons to Sir Stafford Northcote. Sir Michael Hicks Beach had agreed to take the Colonial Office. But when the India Office was offered to Lord Randolph Churchill, he flatly refused to join the Government if Northcote was to continue to lead the House of Commons. Thereupon Sir M. Hicks Beach, regarding Churchill's coöperation in the Government as essential for electioneering purposes, withdrew his own assent.

Sir Stafford, whose health was seriously impaired, might well, in face of such an affront, have decided to hold entirely aloof, but he was persuaded to accept a sinecure office in the new Cabinet with a peerage. Lord Randolph, who had attained his object, agreed to take the India Office — not before he had extorted Lord Salisbury's consent to bestow marks of favour upon his old henchmen, Wolff and Gorst. The latter received the office of Solicitor-General, to which his professional claims were of the slenderest kind.

A more considerable person, Sir Michael Hicks Beach, also had his reward. The edging out of Sir S. Northcote, by the joint action of Lord Randolph and himself, opened the way to his appointment as Chancellor of the Exchequer and Leader of the House of Commons.

CHAPTER XX

THE NEW DEPARTURE (1)

THE " Caretaker " Government came in as a stop-gap until the inevitable general election, on the new franchise and in the redistributed areas, had declared the mind of the country. It was held in November with the result that 335 Liberals were returned, 249 Conservatives and 86 Parnellites. Its two outstanding features were, in Great Britain, the Liberal losses in the boroughs and gains in the counties; and in Ireland the fact that not a single Liberal was returned (as against fourteen in the preceding Parliament). The representation of Ulster was fairly evenly divided — eighteen Nationalists as against seventeen Tories. The eighty-six Nationalists were, however, for all voting purposes in the House of Commons, ciphers under the dictatorship of Parnell.

The Nationalist vote in the British electorate had been given under his directions, almost without exception, to the Conservative as against the Liberal candidates. The reader will remember the promise which Lord R. Churchill records, that Mr. Parnell made to him in their " informal " interview in the summer of 1885.[1] But before the election came in

[1] *See ante,* p. 131.

November, Mr. Parnell had more solid ground for satisfaction with the change of Government.

The " Maamtrasna " debate, almost immediately after the accession of the new Ministry, on Mr. Parnell's motion demanding a fresh inquiry, refused by Lord Spencer, into the case of men who had been convicted of, and executed for, a singularly callous and brutal murder, had momentous consequences. Not only did the new Leader of the House, Sir M. Hicks Beach, in effect, concede the demand, but Lord R. Churchill (who in his character of Indian Secretary had no apparent reason for intervention) cut into the discussion with a crude declaration that he had " no confidence in the Administration of Lord Spencer." Both Mr. Gladstone and Lord Spencer, and (it may be added) the most strenuous of the Liberal Coercionists, Sir W. Harcourt, realized from that moment that in the long and arduous struggle which they had maintained against Irish crime, they were now disavowed — not perhaps by the rank and file — but by the responsible leaders of the Tory Party.

The bribe of the Irish vote in Great Britain at the forthcoming election was a temptation that those leaders could not resist. There have been few less creditable transactions in our parliamentary history.

But the manœuvring of the new Administration did not stop there. Lord Carnarvon — the " Twitters " of Lord Beaconsfield's letters — had been reinstated in the front rank of the Tory Party, and was appointed to succeed Lord Spencer as Viceroy of Ireland. It must have been well known to Lord Salisbury and his colleagues that he was in general sympathy with " Irish aspirations ", and if there had been any doubt about it, it was removed by his first speech in his new office in the House of Lords. By the end of July he arranged a secret meeting between Mr. Parnell and himself in an empty London house. At that interview (as Mr. Churchill happily says) " the two rulers of Ireland — coronetted impotence and uncrowned power — rambled ",[2] over the whole field of Irish self-government!

This curious episode was carefully concealed both by Lord Carnarvon and by Lord Salisbury, who alone were cognisant of it, from the Cabinet, and even from the Leader of the House of Commons; not until two years afterwards (May, 1888) was Lord Salisbury's complicity disclosed.

I cannot recall any other instance of a Prime Minister keeping his most intimate colleague deliberately in the dark in a matter of such vital importance to their common interests. No wonder that Lord Randolph Churchill (when the truth at last came out) " was both astonished and offended at the concealment of such an important political event from Cabinet Ministers by the head of the Government."

Not content with these subterranean pourparlers, Lord Salisbury himself came out (more or less) into the open, and delivered (October 7, 1885) the famous

2 " Churchill ", pp. 361–362.

speech at Newport which was generally interpreted as the signpost to a new departure. It contained (on the Irish problem) two startling and historic declarations. In regard to the future of Irish Government Lord Salisbury, with many reservations as to the " larger organic questions connected with Ireland ", as to which he announced that the Tory Party would not depart from its " traditions ", made this significant statement:

" Local Authorities are more exposed to the temptation of enabling the majority to be unjust to the minority, when they obtain jurisdiction over a small area, than is the case when the Authority derives its sanction and extends its jurisdiction over a wider area. In a large Central Authority the wisdom of several parts of the country will correct the folly and mistakes of one. In a Local Authority that correction is to a much greater extent wanting, and it would be impossible to leave that out of sight in any extension of any such local authority in Ireland."

A formidable plea in favour of Mr. Chamberlain's scheme of a " Central Council " which had been rejected by Mr. Gladstone's Cabinet, against his own advice, in the spring of the year.

But it was in another part of the speech that Lord Salisbury's cynical opportunism found more noteworthy expression. It must be remembered that in the weeks before he spoke there had been a violent recrudescence of boycotting (as well as of other forms of agrarian crime) in Ireland. The Prime Minister toyed with the topic in the tone and after the fashion of an old Saturday Reviewer. Boycotting [3] — he said in substance — is an offence which legislation has very great difficulty in reaching. After all, look at boycotting. An unpopular man, or his family, go to Mass. The congregation with one accord get up and walk out. Are you going to indict people for leaving Church? The plain fact is that boycotting is " more like the excommunication or interdict of the Middle Ages than anything that we know of now." " The truth is, that it depends on the passing humour of the population."

Cold comfort for men and women and children (like the Curtin family at a later date) whose daily lives were being made more like a foretaste of hell than those of the mediæval lepers — coming from the lips of one who was the head, not only of the British Executive, but of the Tory Party — the party from whose traditions, as we have seen, he had told his hearers earlier in the same discourse, you may " rely upon it that we shall not depart."

This speech was the death knell of coercion as an instrument of Irish government, though sporadic attempts were afterwards made, under the auspices of Lord Salisbury himself, with the new war cry (not invented until after the general election of 1885) of " Twenty Years of Resolute Government ", to revive its temporary use.

In one of the intimate conversations which I used to have with Mr. Parnell, at the time when I was his

---

[3] This is from Morley's summarized version of the speech, Vol. III, p. 243.

Counsel before the Special Commission, he once said to me musingly, " It is a great mistake to suppose that Ireland cannot be governed by coercion." It was part — as I thought — of our common creed that that had been proved by this time to be an impossibility, and I told him so. " Perhaps it has," he replied, " but that is not because the task is impossible in itself; it is because, under your English party system, neither party can be trusted to make the policy continuous whatever Government may be in power."

CHAPTER XXI

BUT there was a more important person even than Lord Salisbury upon whose always receptive mind the events of this autumn made an indelible impression. In virtue of his rarely endowed and many-sided temperament, Mr. Gladstone (as is shown at almost every stage of his career) was able, without insincerity or conscious incongruity, to be in turn Idealist and Empiric, and (what is still less common) to be both at the same time. His dealings with the Irish problem are a case in point.

After he had torn up, as he thought, the roots of the " Upas Tree ", between 1869 and 1873, by Disestablishment and the first Land Act — despite the University fiasco — he seems for some years to have given little attention to Irish matters. In a passage already cited, he candidly avows that, as late as the general election of 1880, he had been so absorbed in counterworking Lord Beaconsfield's external policies, that he had no premonitions of the storms which were gathering nearer home. When he became, for the second time, Prime Minister, he found himself confronted in Ireland with a double-faced situation. On the one side, there was organized and open resistance to the law; on the other, there were grievances and wrongs, sanctioned by the law, which, so long as they remained unredressed, weakened and indeed undermined, its moral authority. What was to be done?

The course which he actually took has been already described. It was to assert the law against those who were defying it, and at the same time to purge it, step by step, of the injustices which arrayed the sympathies of a suffering population on the side of anarchy. Coercion and remedial legislation were to go hand in hand, though the balance was constantly being rudely disturbed; and while Mr. Gladstone loyally supported Lord Spencer's firm and impartial use of exceptional powers, he became growingly conscious that this two-sided policy was paradoxical and precarious. With the enfranchisement of the " mud-cabin " voter under the legislation of 1884, and the practical certainty that the Nationalists would enter the next House of Commons with a strength of between eighty and ninety members, the prospect of a continuance of the old system became hopeless. The Crimes Act was about to expire, and (as has been seen) it was the question of its renewal which was the root cause of the disintegration and ultimate downfall of the Gladstone Cabinet in the early months of 1885. The open disavowal of Lord Spencer by the new Government, and the bargaining between it and Mr. Parnell for the Irish vote at the polls, dispelled any remaining doubts; and before the election was actually held it is clear that Mr. Gladstone had made up his mind as to the necessity for a new departure. He gave not a few significant indications of what was in his thoughts in his correspondence with Lord Hartington in the autumn of 1885.[1] It is sufficient to quote from a letter written from Dalmeny on November 10, on the eve of the election:

(Gladstone to Hartington) You have opened a vista which appears to terminate in a possible concession to Ireland of full powers to manage her own local affairs. But I own my leaning to the opinion that if that consummation is in any way to be contemplated, action at a stroke will be more honourable, less unsafe, less uneasy, than the jolting process of a series of partial measures. This is my opinion but I have no intention, as at present advised, of signifying it. I have all along, in public declarations, avoided offering anything to the Nationalists, beyond describing the limiting rule which must govern the question. It is for them to ask, and for us, as I think, to leave the space so defined as open and unencumbered as possible.[2]

It is quite clear, upon a survey of all the contemporary evidence, that the main fear which haunted Mr. Gladstone's mind at this stage was that a situation was perilously imminent in which both political parties would be bargaining for the Irish vote in the House of Commons, each under the temptation to outbid the other. He appealed to the constituencies, throughout the contest, to give the Liberal Party an independent majority. And when the pollings showed that that appeal had been unsuccessful, his first pre-

[1] *See* " Life of Devonshire ", II, 77, *et seq.*
[2] Morley, " Gladstone ", III, 241.

occupation was that, following the precedent of the Franchise negotiations in the previous year, the Tory Government should be " encouraged " to settle the Irish question with such Liberal support as he himself could command. He personally made overtures, which proved abortive, in this sense through Mr. Balfour to Lord Salisbury. Writing many years afterwards (in 1897) he describes what was in his mind:

It has been unreasonably imputed to me that the proposal for Home Rule was a bid for the Irish vote. But my desire for the adjustment of the question by the Tories is surely a conclusive answer. The fact is that I could not rely upon the collective support of the Liberals; but I could, and did, rely upon the support of so many of them as would make the success of the measure certain in the event of its being proposed by the Tory Administration. It would have resembled in substance the Liberal support given to Roman Catholic Emancipation in 1829 and the Repeal of the Corn Laws in 1846. . . . I was therefore by no means eager for the dismissal of the Tory Government, though it counted but 250 supporters out of 670, as long as there were hopes of its taking up the question, or at all events *doing nothing to aggravate the situation.*[3]

The so-called " Hawarden Kite " — a statement in certain organs of the Press of December 17 that Gladstone was contemplating " the establishment of a Parliament in Dublin for dealing with Irish affairs " — was at once disclaimed by Mr. Gladstone himself

[3] Morley, " Gladstone ", III, 284.

as " merely a speculation on his views." But it aroused disquietude and even suspicion in the minds of many of his late colleagues; in none more than in that of Mr. Chamberlain. They were all more or less sore with the feeling that they were being kept in the dark. Curiously enough the one of them to whom Mr. Gladstone directly unbosomed himself at this stage was Lord Hartington, to whom he wrote on December 17 a letter (set out in Morley's " Life ")[4] with authority to show it to Granville and others.

After stating that he has " more or less of opinions and ideas, but no intentions or negotiations ", he declares emphatically his view that " an effort ought to be made *by the Government*[5] without delay " to meet Ireland's demands for the management by an Irish legislative body of Irish as distinct from Imperial affairs. " Only a Government can do it, and a Tory Government can do it more easily and safely than any other." He proceeds to outline the necessary conditions of an " admissible plan " — supremacy of Parliament, protection of minority, etc., etc. He adds that " neither as opinions nor as instructions have I to any one alive promulgated these ideas as decided on by me."

But the whole world believed — no one more firmly than Mr. Chamberlain — that there had been negotiations going on, directly or indirectly, between Gladstone and Parnell, in which the former had definitely committed himself. For the next fortnight

[4] Vol. III, p. 262.   [5] His italics.

or three weeks his colleagues, and none with more persistence than Harcourt, vainly endeavoured to induce him to let them further into his confidence. " It is evident," wrote Chamberlain to Harcourt, " that he proposes to nobble us in detail." [6]

The state of personal relations in the higher ranks of the Liberal Party when the new Parliament was about to meet, in the last week of January, 1886, almost beggars description. Hartington and Chamberlain, at daggers drawn on every other subject, were unconsciously approximating in their common mistrust of the designs of their Chief. Spencer, the " Red Earl " of Nationalist invective, taught by his own unique experience, had finally realized that coercion had become an unworkable policy, and convinced himself that Home Rule was the only alternative. Harcourt who, only two months before, in a phrase which he was not to be allowed to forget, had affirmed that what he desired was " to allow the Tory Government to stew in their own Parnellite juice ", was preparing, with an occasional shiver on the brink, to take the final plunge. And Gladstone himself, in the isolation which he had deliberately chosen, with dwindling, but still not wholly extin-

---

[6] Gardiner, " Harcourt ", I, 558. How far Sir William — though in the cant phrase of the day rapidly " finding Salvation " — still was from a complete state of Grace, is illustrated by a passage in the " Journal ", as late as January 14, 1886, which records an after-dinner conversation at his house. Mr. Gladstone, shocked by his host's flippancy on what was becoming to him the most sacred of all mundane subjects, turned to him indignantly and said: " You think Ireland is a little hell on earth." W. V. H.: " Yes, I think the only mistake Cromwell ever made was when he offered them the alternative of Connaught."

guished hopes, was waiting and watching for the Government to define their policy.

That policy was at last made clear. On January 26, the Leader of the House of Commons declared their intention at once to introduce a new batch of coercive measures, which was to be followed in due course, after the approved fashion, by a Land Bill, developing and extending the machinery of purchase.

The result of this announcement, Mr. Gladstone writes in the memorandum of 1897 already cited, was that " my rule of action was changed at once, and I determined on taking any and every legitimate opportunity to remove the existing Government from office." He immediately communicated his intentions to Sir William Harcourt, who exclaimed, " What! Are you prepared to go forward without either Hartington or Chamberlain? " " I answered ' Yes.' I believe it was in my mind to say, if I did not actually say it, that I was prepared to go forward without anybody. . . . This was one of the great imperial occasions which call for such resolutions." [7]

A more momentous resolution was probably never taken by a man who had passed his seventy-sixth birthday. It is not an exaggeration to say that it changed the whole course of British politics during the lifetime of a generation.

[7] Morley, " Gladstone ", III, 287–288.

CHAPTER XXII

END OF THE SALISBURY GOVERNMENT

THE result of the election of 1885, if it gave Mr. Gladstone cause for much meditation, was almost equally perturbing to the Salisbury Government.

Lord R. Churchill, when he saw how the polls were going, was strongly in favour of an immediate coalition with the " Whigs ", even offering to give up his own place to make more room for them. He pressed that course at the end of November on Lord Salisbury, who replied that the time for coalition had not come yet, and caustically remarked that " they (the Whigs) hate me as much as they hate you — and if retirements are required for the sake of repose and Whig combinations, I shall claim to retire with you." [1]

Lord Randolph returned to the charge. There were three possible methods, he said, which he placed in the following order: (1) the (immediate) offer of places in the Government to the Whigs, (2) the production of a " large genuine and liberal programme ", (3) after production, and some measure of prosecution, of the programme, the renewal of the offer of places in the Government. The " large and liberal "

[1] " Churchill ", p. 431.

programme [2] is a voluminous document, in which neither coercion nor Home Rule finds a place. Indeed, its author expressly declares his opinion that coercion is impossible " *now* ", and " anything in the nature of an Irish Parliament is impossible *always*."

Lord Salisbury's answer is highly characteristic. In composing the Queen's speech (for he dismisses the idea of immediate resignation) he says that " he entirely agrees that our leaning must be to the Moderate Liberals." But we should " take note of the fact that the moment for bargaining with them has not yet come." . . . " The extra tinge of Liberalism in our policy will be part of the bargain when it comes, and must not be given away before that time comes. If we *are too free with our cash now we shall have no money to go to market with when the market is open*." Lord Randolph had suggested as an item in the " large and liberal programme " the abolition of primogeniture. On which Lord Salisbury, who was never at a loss for a cynical metaphor, makes the comment that " the abolition of primogeniture is in itself of no importance except on *strategic* grounds; it is not worth the trouble of resistance. But it is a bit of a flag. The concession would be distasteful to a certain number of our people now, and it might be acceptable as a *wedding present* to the Moderate Liberals, whenever the Conservative Party leads them to the altar." [3]

[2] Set out at length in " Churchill ", pp. 433 *et sq*.

[3] *Ibid*., pp. 437–438. In the same vein he favours the splitting up of London for Local Government purposes. " The multiplication of Municipalities would please the local leaders, who hope to figure in them, and become Mayors."

Lord Randolph, in his rejoinder, rivals his Chief
in candour, but continues to dissent from his dilatory
tactics. He is for " opening the market " without delay. " If " (he writes), " I apprehended your meaning rightly, you would make your programme rather
rigidly orthodox Tory, with a view of expanding it
into Whig heresy when the time for a fusion should
seem to have arrived. Now I hold very strongly that
in that case the moment for a fusion will never
arrive." (The actual " wedding " was not in fact,
formally celebrated till ten years later — in 1895.)
He also resorts to metaphor to drive home his point:
" It is by showing your hand — by showing how
many good trumps you have in it, that you will gain
support. It is by hiding your hand, by giving cause
for the belief . . . that you have no trumps, that
you will lose support." . . . " Our task should be to
keep the boroughs as well as to win the counties; this
can only be done by an active, progressive — I risk
the word, a democratic — policy: a casting off and a
burning of those old, worn-out aristocratic and class
garments from which the Derby-Dizzy lot " (Shade
of Lord Beaconsfield!) " with their following of
county families could never, or never cared to, extri-
cate themselves." [4]

A picturesque and edifying correspondence. Lord
Salisbury had his way.

There were, it would seem, not a few Conservatives who were in favour (as was Mr. Gladstone) of
attempting to arrive at a settlement of the Irish ques-

[4] " Churchill."

tion by coöperation between the two great English parties. This, however, was a policy to which Lord Randolph (for the time being at any rate), as well as Lord Salisbury, was strenuously opposed. " The Disraeli epoch of constant metamorphoses of principles and party has passed away " — he writes grandiloquently to Chief Justice Morris — " Radical work must be done by Radical artists." [5] His party having had the full benefit — such as it was — of the Parnellite vote in Great Britain at the elections — it was variously estimated at the time to have been worth to the Tories from twenty to forty seats — his face was now resolutely set against Home Rule. When the " Hawarden Kite " was flown, Mr. Gardiner tells us that Churchill was reported to have said, *à propos* of whether the Tory Government would proceed with Home Rule: " Oh, no, we will have nothing to do with Home Rule of any kind now: we have got Gladstone pinned to it; we will make him expose his scheme in the House of Commons. Let him defeat us with the aid of the Parnellites, and then let us dissolve and go to the country with the cry of ' The Empire in Danger '." [6] He appears even to have authorized Mr. Labouchere to tell Mr. Gladstone that he would urge Ulster to resist Home Rule by arms.

Meanwhile Lord Carnarvon, face to face with the daily growing domination of the National League in Ireland, had announced to his colleagues that (in Mr. Churchill's words) " unless the Cabinet could move in the direction of Home Rule he could not

[5] " Churchill ", p. 446.　　[6] Gardiner, " Harcourt ", I, 550.

continue their servant." His resignation and that of his Chief Secretary, Sir William Hart Dyke, soon became public. The Cabinet were at first divided upon the expediency of proceeding at once with coercive proposals, and an ambiguous and non-committal paragraph on the subject was inserted in the Queen's speech. Mr. W. H. Smith was hastily appointed Chief Secretary, and was sent over to Dublin — as was said at the time — to " discover a policy." But the Cabinet could not wait for his report and announced in the House of Commons (as has been already stated) on January 26, their intention at once to introduce repressive measures.

The same evening the Government were defeated by a majority of seventy-nine on Mr. Jesse Collings' " Three Acres and a Cow " amendment to the address. Hartington and Chamberlain spoke and voted on opposite sides. Eighteen Liberals voted against the amendment, and seventy-six were absent, including Mr. Bright. Mr. Gladstone voted for it, as did the Parnellites.

Lord Salisbury at once resigned.

CHAPTER XXIII

FIRST STAGE OF HOME RULE

Mr. GLADSTONE accepted without hesitation the Queen's commission to form a Government, and thus entered upon the third and briefest of his four terms of office as Prime Minister. (February–July, 1886.)

The basis of his new Administration, as defined by himself in a memorandum, which was shown to all whom he asked to be his colleagues in the Cabinet, was " to examine whether it is or is not practicable to comply with the desire widely prevalent in Ireland, and testified by the return of 85 out of 103 representatives, for the establishment by statute of a Legislative Body to sit in Dublin and to deal with Irish as distinguished from Imperial affairs." Acceptance of such an invitation would not in itself involve more than a willingness to take part in the inquiry; not, of course, as a mere academic exploration; but with the restraints and obligations of Cabinet responsibility. It was in that sense (not without many misgivings) that Mr. Chamberlain and Mr. Trevelyan agreed, in the first instance, to join the Government.[1]

[1] Dilke, who might have been an important personal factor, was for the time out of action.

Not so Lord Hartington, to whom Mr. Gladstone appears to have been the first to reply. To him it seemed that, unless such an " examination " was intended to result in a concrete " proposal ", it would only make matters worse. And while he chivalrously and publicly acquitted Mr. Gladstone personally of anything in the nature of a sudden *volte-face,* he no doubt felt that no " proposal " was in the least likely to be evolved to which he himself could honestly assent.

In the result a Cabinet was formed without most of the leading Whigs, but mainly of old materials. The only newcomers were Lord Herschell, Mr. Campbell-Bannerman, Mr. Mandella (all of whom had held office outside the Cabinet in Mr. Gladstone's Second Administration) and Mr. Morley, to whom was assigned the vitally important post of Chief Secretary for Ireland. Lord Rosebery became for the first time Foreign Secretary.

Mr. Chamberlain was offered, in the first instance, the curiously inappropriate office of First Lord of the Admiralty, which he not unnaturally refused, and then the Local Government Board, which he accepted. As he was undoubtedly the second person in power and influence in the new Government, it remains to this day inexplicable that the Prime Minister should not have given him his choice of office. The personal situation was not improved by a tactless proposal (ultimately dropped) to make a petty reduction in the salary of his devoted henchman, Mr. Collings, who became his Parliamentary Secretary.

The really important post of Home Secretary was
given to Mr. Childers, without whom it was one of
Mr. Gladstone's foibles to think that no Liberal
Cabinet was adequately equipped.

While the new Government, or rather its Head,
was pursuing the " examination ", its opponents were
not idle. The forefront of the stage was occupied by
Lord R. Churchill. In a private letter to his intimate
friend, the Irish Lord Justice Fitzgibbon, he writes:
" I decided some time ago that, if the G.O.M. went
for Home Rule, the Orange Card would be the one
to play." As a first move in the game he went over
to Belfast, and in an inflammatory harangue declared
that " the struggle was not likely to remain within
the lines of what we are accustomed to look upon as
Constitutional action." And he supplemented this
revolutionary suggestion in a letter to a correspondent, in which he used a phrase which became the
battle cry of the Orangemen: " Ulster at the proper
moment will resort to the supreme arbitrament of
force: *Ulster will fight: Ulster will be right."*

He was more anxious than ever for a real and
immediate coalition. At a great demonstration at
Manchester he urged, in language which has received
the conscious or unconscious flattery of imitation in
these latter days, the " formation of a New Party,
containing all that is best in the politics of Tory,
Liberal and Whig." It was upon this occasion that
he invented for the opponents and supporters of
Home Rule the two question-begging labels of
Unionist and Separatist. Lord Salisbury continued

for a time to throw cold water upon the suggestion of fusion. Neither he nor the "Whigs" had yet got over their deep-seated dislike and distrust of one another. He compared Lord Hartington and his associates to the Peelites, who "were always putting themselves up to auction, and always buying themselves in. That seems" (he adds) "the Whig idea at present."[2]

But as passions rapidly developed, as they did with a bitterness, not only political, but social and personal, hitherto almost unknown in Victorian politics, this attitude of reciprocal coyness completely broke down. On April 14 (the day after the first reading of the Home Rule Bill) a demonstration was held at the Opera House, at which Lord Salisbury and Lord Hartington appeared and performed on the same stage. There was a large attendance of Whig peers, and some eminent Liberal Commoners like Mr. Goschen.[3] Lord Salisbury, with bland audacity, in view of the events of the preceding summer and autumn, declared that what was wanted in Ireland was a "firm, wise, and continuous administration of the law" — an idea which he crystallized a month later at St. James' Hall (in a speech in which he incidentally remarked that "you would not confide free institutions to Hottentots") into a phrase which became famous: "Twenty years of resolute Government." Mr. Goschen, descending from his usually

[2] "Churchill", p. 485.
[3] Two conspicuous absentees were Mr. Chamberlain (who had already resigned) and Lord R. Churchill, who described the meeting as a "piece of premature gush."

high level of dignity and common sense, made his
audience first shiver with alarm, and then work themselves into a frenzy of vicarious heroism, as he drew
a picture of the " desperadoes who bore some little
part in lifting the curtain which hid the form of
' Justice to Ireland ' . . . at their cruel work again."
. . . Some say " the dagger may again be brought
into use. If so, we shall make our wills and do our
duty."

Mr. Gladstone never spared himself; never less
than in these months, when in his seventy-seventh
year he essayed the task of both architect and builder
of a new Constitution. It was indeed the final turn-
ing point in his career, and from this time onwards,
during nearly ten years, the Irish cause became to
him a religion. The unique array of his varied gifts
— constructive, dialectical, strategic — was never so
strikingly illustrated as when they were fused in the
Apostolic fervour of a new Crusade.[4]

It was not till five or six weeks after the formation
of the Government that the Prime Minister (March
13) produced to the Cabinet for the first time the two
Bills — a Home Rule Bill, and a Land Purchase Bill
— which with immense industry he had evolved.
Unfortunately, as his warmest admirers must think,
in the process of preparation he had not taken Mr.
Chamberlain into his confidence. As produced, both
measures were found unacceptable by him and by
Mr. Trevelyan, and the two Ministers at a later

[4] An " old Parliamentary hand " was the description which he gave
of himself in his first speech in the House of Commons in this memorable
session.

Cabinet (March 26) resigned their offices. Their objections it is not necessary to enumerate here,[5] and grave and even formidable as some of them were, it seems probable that, as regards the Home Rule Bill, they might, in a less strained atmosphere of personal relations, have been to a large extent, if not wholly, met. The Land Bill was doomed from the first; apart from Lord Spencer and Mr. Morley, it had only lukewarm support from Mr. Gladstone's colleagues in the Cabinet; and, as I can testify from personal observation, in many parts of the country it had more to do with the crushing defeat of the Government in the general election of July than the Home Rule Bill itself. Mr. Chamberlain used to boast that he had been a Home Ruler long before Mr. Gladstone; he was the author, the previous year, of the proposal for a National Council in Ireland in which (as has been seen) he had the support of the Prime Minister, who deplored the adverse attitude to it of the majority of the then Cabinet; and the provision in the Bill of 1886, which was to him the most obnoxious of all — the exclusion of the Irish members from the Imperial Parliament — was for all practical purposes dropped before the second reading.

Lord Morley, in his " Recollections ", describes how, after a dinner at Marlborough House six years later — in 1892 — " Rosebery and Chamberlain were discussing the disruption of the Cabinet in 1886, and beckoned me to join them. Chamberlain said that when he went into the Cabinet on the morning

[5] They are set out in "Gladstone", III, 302.

of March 26 he had no notion of breaking away, but that Mr. Gladstone, on the contrary, had gone into it that morning with his mind made up to drive him out. Rosebery shared Chamberlain's impression. They wished to know mine. I said mine was much the same."

It is in this way that it often happens that history is made or marred.

CHAPTER XXIV

THE FIRST HOME RULE BILL (1886)

MR. CHAMBERLAIN'S position in the weeks
which followed his resignation bristled with difficulties which might have daunted a man of less courage
and self-confidence. He had literally nothing in common with the Whig seceders, with whom it seemed
he must now perforce cast in his lot. During the
election contest of the autumn, though he had not
spared Lord Salisbury, Lord Hartington and Mr.
Goschen had been the favourite targets for his invective. The " Caucus " — his own creation — now
repudiated him, and his chosen organizer, Mr.
Schnadhorst of Birmingham, in whose astuteness and
resource both friends and opponents had an almost
superstitious belief, was heart and soul with Mr. Gladstone.

The man who tried the hardest both to smooth his
path and to stiffen his attitude was Lord R. Churchill,
who at once sought to establish intimate relations
with him. This was not so difficult as from their prolonged and uncompromising hostility in the past
might at first sight appear. As Mr. Churchill truly,
if somewhat naïvely, says: [1] " Their moods and ways

[1] " Churchill ", p. 487.

THE RIGHT HON. JOSEPH
CHAMBERLAIN

of looking at things — to some extent their methods — were not altogether dissimilar." To put the thing more crudely, they were both born and highly trained demagogues. Their " close and cordial coöperation " advanced so rapidly that by the end of March Lord Randolph had succeeded in getting Lord Salisbury home from the Riviera, and arranging a meeting between him and Mr. Chamberlain on the " neutral ground " of the Turf Club. There does not appear to be any authentic record of what passed at this, the first personal introduction of the two men, each of whom had in his time accused the other of almost every imaginable political crime.[2]

The two twin Bills were successively submitted for first reading in the House of Commons early in April. There was no division upon either. The Land Bill found few friends in any quarter, and made no further parliamentary progress, though its unpalatable, and for the most part unpopular, provisions furnished useful ammunition in the outside agitation against Home Rule. The debate on the Home Rule Bill at this stage does not call for detailed notice, as it is overshadowed in interest and importance by that on the second reading. The two most damaging attacks in the preliminary skirmish came from Lord Hartington, who, among all the assailants of the scheme, now and throughout the controversy, made by far the deepest impression both upon the House

---

[2] The compulsory abstention at this time of Sir C. Dilke from active politics may (as is suggested by his biographers) have facilitated the Churchill-Chamberlain *rapprochement*.

of Commons and the country; and from Mr. Goschen, who, in the judgment of Mr. Gladstone, " supplied, in the main, soul, brains, and movement to the
dissentient body of Liberals."

In the interval between the first and second read-
ings a fierce campaign was carried on in the country.
The utmost use was made by the opponents of the
Bill of Mr. Gladstone's own description (not yet five
years old) of the Nationalists as " marching through
rapine to the dismemberment of the Empire " ; and
of a phrase, which it was discovered that Parnell had
once used to a Fenian audience in America, about
" snapping the last link " that bound Ireland to Great
Britain. In London every form of lobbying and wire-
pulling was in full activity. The social boycott of the
Gladstonians was carried to such lengths that the
Prime Minister was seriously afraid lest he should be
unable to find guests for his dinner table on the
official celebration of the Queen's birthday.[3] " If
Hartington," he wrote to a friend, " were to get up
and move a vote of want of confidence after dinner,
he would almost carry it."

The debate on the second reading of the Home
Rule Bill opened on May 10, and ran on for twelve
parliamentary days. It was sustained throughout at
a high level. Mr. Gladstone's winding-up speech may
be studied with interest and profit as a masterpiece,
which exhibits all the arts of the most consummate
parliamentarian of his own or perhaps of any time.[4]

[3] Morley, " Gladstone ", III, 322.
[4] Two salient and vividly contrasted passages are to be found in

But it was not the debate which determined the Division. The fortunes of the Bill wavered and flickered day by day, and were ultimately settled behind the scenes. At one time, after a meeting of the Liberal Party at the Foreign Office (May 27) at which Mr. Gladstone declared himself ready to consider plans for the retention of the Irish members (the Chamberlain *cheval de bataille*) and to " hang up " the Bill after the second reading, it seemed as if the situation had been saved. But the manœuvre did not survive a couple of hours of merciless dissection in the House of Commons. The waverers again hardened their hearts to settled hostility, and the final and fatal blow was prepared at a meeting of some fifty-five Liberal members, presided over by Mr. Chamberlain (May 31). A resolution to oppose the second reading was passed in the end with practical unanimity.

This result was attributed at the time to a letter from Mr. Bright, which was read by Mr. Chamberlain to the meeting and which has been described as the " death warrant of the Bill." It is an historical document of so much importance that it deserves to be given *in extenso*. Mr. Bright, it must be remembered, had not taken part in any of the debates. The last speech he ever made in the House was on the election of Speaker at the beginning of the session of 1886. The letter was as follows:

Morley, " Gladstone ", III, 338–340. Sir Richard Temple records in his " Life in Parliament " : " In the last twenty minutes or so, I have never heard such oratory anywhere from any man." The peroration is set out in the note at the end of this chapter.

MY DEAR CHAMBERLAIN, — My present intention is to vote against the Second Reading. Not having spoken in the debate I am not willing to have my view of the Bill or Bills in any doubt. But I am not willing to take the responsibility of advising others as to their course. If they can content themselves with abstaining from the Division, I shall be glad. They will render a greater service by preventing the threatened Dissolution than by compelling it, if Mr. Gladstone is unwise enough to venture upon it. You will see from this exactly where I am. A small majority for the Bill may be almost as good as its defeat, and may save the country from the heavy sacrifice of a General Election. I wish I could join you, but I cannot now change the path I have taken from the beginning of this unhappy discussion. Believe me always, sincerely yours,

JOHN BRIGHT.

P.S. — If you think it of any use you may read this note to your friends.

Nobody seems to have been more surprised than Mr. Bright himself when he heard of the decision of the meeting, which was apparently the exact opposite of what he desired.

" My note," he wrote to Mr. Chamberlain, " was intended to make it more easy for you and your friends to abstain from voting in the coming Division." And that surely is the construction which the ordinary man, reading it now for the first time, would put upon it. This is another of the series of *malentendus* with which the history of an eventful year is so plentifully strewn.

When the Division came to be taken (June 8) the numbers were 313 for the Bill: 343 (including 93 Liberals) against: an adverse majority of 30.

The Cabinet met the next day to find Mr. Gladstone ready (as Lord Morley tells us) with *twelve* reasons for dissolution as against resignation, which appear to have completely submerged the protests of a small dissentient minority. The Queen gave her assent, and the shortest Parliament of her reign came to an end.

NOTE

The final passage in Mr. Gladstone's closing speech in the debate on the second reading of the Home Rule Bill (June 8, 1886):

" You have power, you have wealth, you have rank, you have station, you have organization, you have the place of power. What have we? We think that we have the people's heart; and we believe, and we know, we have the promise of the harvest of the future. As to the people's heart, you may dispute it, and dispute it with perfect sincerity. Let that matter make its own proof. As to the harvest of the future, I doubt if you have so much confidence, and I believe that there is in the breast of many a man who means to vote against us to-night, a profound misgiving, approaching even to a deep conviction, that the end will be as we foresee, and not as you — that the ebbing tide is with you, and the flowing tide is with us.

" Ireland stands at your bar, expectant, hopeful,

almost suppliant. Her words are the words of truth and soberness. She asks a blessed oblivion of the past, and in that oblivion our interest is deeper than even hers. My right honourable friend (Mr. Goschen) asks us to-night to abide by the traditions of which we are the heirs. What traditions? By the Irish traditions? Go into the length and breadth of the world, ransack the literature of all the countries; find, if you can, a single voice, a single book — find, I would almost say, as much as a single newspaper article, unless the product of the day, in which the conduct of England towards Ireland is anywhere treated except with profound and bitter condemnation. Are these the traditions to which we are exhorted to stand? No, they are a sad exception to the glory of our country. They are a broad, and black blot upon the pages of its history, and what we want to do is to stand by the traditions of which we are the heirs, in all matters except our relations to Ireland, and to make our relations to Ireland conform to the other traditions of our country. So I hail the demand of Ireland for what I call a blessed oblivion of the past. She asks also a boon for the future; and that boon for the future, unless we are much mistaken, will be a boon to us in respect of honour no less than a boon to her in respect of happiness, prosperity and peace. Such, Sir, is her prayer.

" Think, I beseech you — think well, think wisely, think not for a moment but for the years that are to come, before you reject this Bill."

CHAPTER XXV

THE CLIMAX OF CHURCHILL (1886)

THE Dissentient Liberal members whose votes defeated the Bill and forced the Dissolution belonged, for the most part, to the Right Wing of the party whose natural leader was Lord Hartington, though Birmingham, where the Bright-Chamberlain influence was supreme, and some other constituencies of Radical traditions, gave Mr. Chamberlain a following of his own. Moreover, the supposed menace to the Ulster Protestants, of which the most was made on the platform by Churchill and Chamberlain himself, had a disintegrating effect upon what had hitherto been the most stalwart section of the Liberal Party — the Nonconformists; some of their most eminent clergy, Dale, Spurgeon, and others, betook themselves, sadly and reluctantly, to the Unionist camp. Mr. Gladstone undoubtedly believed that he was confronted with what was to all intents and purposes a " Whig revolt "; he was confident that the bulk of his party, and of the rank and file of the electorate, was behind him; he put into currency the famous antithesis between the " Classes " and the " Masses " ; and described the appeal to the country (due, according to Churchill, to the " boundless egotism of an old man in a hurry ") as a " People's Dissolution."

The result of the election was to reduce the Ministerial Liberals (or Gladstonians, as they came to be called) in the new House from 235 to 196, to reduce the Dissentient Liberals (or Liberal Unionists, as they henceforward called themselves) to 74, and to increase the Conservatives from 251 to 316. As the Parnellites remained at their old figure, while no single party had an independent majority of its own, the two Unionist groups in combination exceeded the rest of the House by 110. The votes actually polled in Great Britain were almost evenly divided between the supporters and the opponents of Home Rule.

Mr. Gladstone resigned (July 30), and after some parleyings (which came to nothing) as to the possibilities of an official coalition between the two sections of the majority, Lord Salisbury again became Prime Minister. He invited Sir M. Hicks Beach to continue to be leader of the party in the House of Commons, a post which he had filled with efficiency and resourcefulness in the preceding session. Sir Michael declined, for reasons which are best given in his own language in after years: " I felt that Lord Randolph Churchill was superior in eloquence, ability and influence to myself; that the position of Leader in name but not in fact would be intolerable." (He no doubt had fresh in his memory the sad experiences of Sir Stafford Northcote.) " And that it was better for the party and the country that the Leader in fact should be Leader also in name. Lord Salisbury very strongly pressed me to remain, saying that character was of most importance, and quoting Lord Althorp as an instance; but I insisted. . . ."[1] Lord Salisbury was no doubt perfectly sincere, though one may be permitted to wonder whether this was the most tactful way of handling a delicate matter. It brings to mind the reported remark of Queen Victoria, when, after Lord Westbury's resignation, she handed the Great Seal for the second time to Lord Cranworth. " You see, Lord Cranworth, how much better it is to be good than to be clever."

Sir Michael adds that it took him a considerable time (" more than half an hour ") to overcome the modest hesitations of Lord Randolph, who was at last persuaded to undertake the double functions of Chancellor of the Exchequer and Leader of the House. Hicks Beach himself magnanimously agreed to accept the most thankless office in the whole Administration — that of Chief Secretary for Ireland. It may be of interest to record a casual remark which, many years afterwards, Lord Randolph one day made to me at the dinner table, that " all through, the old, and not the young, Tories had been his best friends ", and that " it was Hicks Beach and the Duke of Rutland who had made him Leader of the House of Commons."

For the rest, with one exception, the new Ministry was little more than a replica of the Conservative Government which had resigned six months before.

[1] " Churchill ", p. 527.

The exception was a remarkable one. Mr. Henry Matthews, who had just been elected as a Conservative against a Gladstonian Liberal in one of the divisions of Birmingham, was, at Lord R. Churchill's solicitations, and to the universal surprise of the whole Tory Party, appointed Home Secretary. He was a Roman Catholic, and a distinguished member of the English Bar, who had sat for a short time in Parliament many years before for a small Irish borough as a Nationalist of a somewhat extreme type. He had to vacate his seat at Birmingham on accepting office, and his only chance of reëlection lay in combining the support of the Radical Unionists with that of the Tories in the constituency. Mr. Chamberlain was placed for a moment in a highly embarrassing situation, but he finally succumbed to a fusillade of appeals from Lord Randolph. The necessary marching orders were given, and the new Home Secretary was returned unopposed. " I am delighted," wrote Lord Randolph to Mr. Chamberlain. " I expect the Midland Conservative Club will put up a statue to you, which I shall have to unveil." [2] It was close upon the second anniversary of the Aston Riots.

It may be added here that Mr. Matthews' subsequent career reflected little credit on Lord Randolph's discernment. Both as a debater, and as an administrator, the only impression he left upon the House of Commons was that of a clever man who had lost his way.[3] In private he had much personal

---

[2] " Churchill ", p. 534.

[3] A typical illustration was the once famous case of Miss Cass. The

charm, and a good deal of rather recondite culture.
At the Bar he had had a large practice, and a position
of his own; one of his latest forensic achievements
before taking office was his sensational cross-examination of the leading personage in the *cause célèbre*
of the day. But his was another case to be added to a
long list — from the name of Erskine downwards —
of great advocates who have been great parliamentary
failures.[4]

I am able to speak with first-hand knowledge of
the House of Commons which sat from 1886 to 1892.
I had been for some years a convinced Home Ruler,
and was not one of those who (as Campbell-Bannerman said to a popular and much-caricatured colleague) " found salvation " in the early months of
1886. At the Dissolution in July, I resolved to run
the risks — which are formidable to a young barrister
with a moderate practice — of becoming a candidate,
and at the suggestion of my close friend, Mr. Haldane, who had been returned for East Lothian in the
previous November, I presented myself in that
character to the electors of East Fife. The sitting
Member, Mr. Boyd Kinnear, was a local laird, an
accomplished man, and a political writer of some

Home Secretary had quite a good defence, which he so mishandled that
the Government suffered a defeat. The vote which I gave on that occasion is one of the few of which I am inclined to be ashamed.

4 Of the famous leaders of the English Bar in my younger days —
Charles Russell, Davey, Rigby, Edward Clarke — only one, the last-
named, became a first-rate House of Commons man. Another exception
came from the Scottish Bar — Mr. J. P. B. Robertson — afterwards a
Lord of Appeal, who was more than once put up by his Party to follow
Mr. Gladstone in a full-dress encounter.

distinction; he belonged to the Chamberlain wing of
the party, and had voted against the second reading
of the Home Rule Bill. I had the disadvantage of
being wholly unknown to the electorate, and an
Englishman to boot, but after a short and sharp contest, in which the Land Bill [5] gave me more trouble
than Home Rule, I won the seat by a small but adequate majority. I continued to hold it without inter-
ruption for the following thirty-two years.

Mr. George Curzon — afterwards Lord Curzon of
Kedleston — was also returned for the first time at
this election. He and I always sat upon opposite sides
of the House, but we formed a friendship which, I
am glad to say, survived the rubs and shocks of
public life. I soon found myself a member of a small
group of young men — Sir E. Grey, Haldane, Arthur
Acland, Sydney Buxton, Tom Ellis — who sat, and
more or less acted, together in what was equivalent
to the " Mountain " in the French Convention, and
came to be regarded with some suspicion as " advanced " and " dangerous ", and inclined to mutiny,
by the orthodox and experienced greybeards of the
Party. Our favourite mentor on the Front Bench was
Mr. John Morley (not one of the " greybeards "),
with whom, during the whole of this Parliament, we
came to be on terms of growing intimacy and confidence. Let me add here a tribute which (later on)
our mentor was good enough to pay us: " Since 1886

[5] Mr. Morley reports to Sir W. Harcourt in April, 1890, a conversation which he had just had with Mr. Gladstone, who " spoke bitterly
of the Land Bill of 1886 as the worst political failure he had ever associated himself with." (Gardiner, II, 116.)

had sprung up, among a younger generation of Liberals, a small new group that was destined as time went on to exert much influence for good or evil on the fortunes of their country. They were a working alliance, not a school; they had idealism but were no Utopians. Haldane, Asquith, Grey, Acland, had the temper of men of the world, and the temper of business. They had conscience, character, and took their politics to heart." [6]

The short autumn session of the new House (August–September, 1886) will always be memorable to those who attended it, as it saw the beginning, and what proved to be the end, of the brief and brilliant leadership of Lord R. Churchill. He was far from happy. As he wrote to Lord Hartington (September 13): " The position of this Government must always be most precarious. It may have a long life, but it is a rickety infant, requiring the most careful handling. . . . I feel awfully alone in the House of Commons, and am glad to grasp an opportunity of placing things before you as I look at them." [7] His loneliness, and almost ostentatious aloofness from his colleagues on the Treasury Bench, was, indeed, obvious night after night to any clear-sighted observer. But under much provocation he kept his temper well under control, and the Queen was well justified when, in her letter to him at the end of the session, she congratulated him on having " shown much skill and judgment in his Leadership." Of his few pronounce-

[6] Morley's Recollections ", I, 323.
[7] " Churchill ", pp. 545–546.

ments in this short session on general policy, one only still survives: a dictum, much applauded at the time, and not, perhaps, more short-sighted than many other " intelligent anticipations " : " The great sign-posts of our policy are equality, similarity, and, if I may use such a word, simultaneity of treatment, so far as is practicable, in the development of a genu-inely popular system of government in all the four countries which form the United Kingdom." [8]

[8] August 19, 1886.

CHAPTER XXVI

PERIPETEIA (1886–1887)

LORD R. CHURCHILL was not content to be merely Leader of the House of Commons. Parliament had scarcely adjourned when he made it clear, in two speeches delivered in the country to large and representative Conservative gatherings at Dartford and Bradford, that he was prepared to take upon himself to prescribe and promulgate the policy, domestic, foreign and financial, of the Government. It was, according to his statement of it, to be a frankly democratic policy all round. It included not only (in substance) the rural programme of Mr. Jesse Collings, which had led earlier in the year to the downfall of Lord Salisbury's first Administration, but also — what was regarded in those days by the bulk of the Tory Party in Parliament as a pernicious and revolutionary innovation — the adoption in the House of Commons, as an integral part of its procedure, of Closure by a simple majority. Mr. Churchill declares that the daring and comprehensive projects which his father foreshadowed in these speeches, had " received the consent of the Cabinet."[1] If so, his colleagues must have been under the tem-

---

[1] " Churchill ", p. 559.

porary sway of some form of hypnotism, from which, even before his presence was removed, they speedily began to awake. There is a closer approximation to the real facts in the same writer's later statement that " discord stirred restlessly behind the curtains of Cabinet secrecy ", and that the autumn councils of Ministers were " not harmonious whether upon foreign or domestic affairs." [2] Lord Salisbury, at the end of an ineffectual attempt to bring his colleagues to an agreement on one of the most prominent items in the Dartford programme, appears to have written to his Chancellor of the Exchequer, with his usual frankness, " I wish there were no such thing as Local Government." [3] " Alas," wrote the Chancellor of the Exchequer to the Prime Minister in November, " I see the Dartford programme crumbling into pieces every day. I am afraid it is an idle schoolboy's dream to suppose that Tories can legislate — as I did, stupidly." [4] Lord Salisbury replied in his best vein, with an instructive discourse, on the relation of his party to the " Classes " and " Masses " : " I think the Classes and the dependents of Class are the strongest ingredients in our composition, but we have so to conduct our legislation that we shall give *some satisfaction* [5] to both Classes and Masses. This is specially difficult with the Classes — because all legislation is rather unwelcome to them — as tending to disturb a state of things with which they are satisfied."

[2] " Churchill ", p. 603.
[3] *Ibid.*
[4] *Ibid.*, p. 606.
[5] The italics are mine.

He goes on to point out the danger of a Tory
Government producing " drastic symmetrical measures, hitting the Classes hard ", in the hope that the
" democratic forces will carry you through." " I
think," he adds, " that such a policy will fail. I do
not mean that the ' Classes ' will join issue with you
on one of the measures which hits them hard, and
beat you on that. That is not the way they fight.
They will select some other matter on which they can
appeal to prejudice, and on which they think the
Masses will be indifferent; and on that they will
upset you." [6]

Who can fail to admire the serpentine wisdom of
the older man? But Lord Randolph (who was still
only thirty-seven) had not outgrown — with all his
waywardness — the faculties of hope and enthusiasm, and refused to be taught.

The truth is that, until the admission to the inner
circle in November of Mr. A. J. Balfour, who was
already Secretary for Scotland, Churchill had not a
single real friend in the Cabinet. There were even
serious and growing differences between himself and
Hicks Beach on critical matters of Irish policy. He
made no secret of his disapproval of Lord Iddesleigh's conduct of foreign affairs in the east of
Europe. He had ridden roughshod over so many
obstacles, brushing aside in his rapid ascent this man
and that who seemed to stand in his way, and he was
at such little pains to disguise the contempt which he
felt for not a few of his colleagues, that the isolation

[6] " Churchill ", p. 607.

in which he found himself, at the very top of his career, was an inevitable result for which he had largely himself to thank.

While, under these discouraging conditions, he was still trying his best to save from the daws and the kites the mangled remnants of the Dartford menu, there was another direction in which he found a still more congenial field for his restless and insatiable activities. Probably no one has ever entered upon the office of Chancellor of the Exchequer who was less familiar with the details, and even the rudimentary technique, of finance. Amusing stories were current of his early encounters with the experienced Treasury officials, brought up in the straightest Gladstonian school, and steeped to a man in the principles and methods which the greatest of modern Finance Ministers had inculcated and practised. There was much fluttering of wings in that austere dovecote at the advent of this irreverent and callow novice. But in a very few weeks he had conquered their prejudices, and even captured their respect and good will, by the rapidity of his intelligence, his unaffected willingness to be taught, and his unwearying industry. Once he had mastered the difference between a decimal point and a full stop, he progressed by leaps and bounds in his new studies, and the autumn was not far advanced when he was laying down the lines of a comprehensive and ambitious Democratic Budget.

That Budget, all the prospective details of which are to be found in Mr. Churchill's " Life ", was never presented to Parliament. The " blind Fury with the

abhorred shears " was lying in wait for it from the
first. The actual, or, at any rate, the ostensible,
cause which precipitated an inevitable crisis was the
refusal of Mr. W. H. Smith and Lord G. Hamilton
to make the reductions which the Chancellor of the
Exchequer demanded in the Army and Navy Estimates. They were backed by Lord Salisbury. Lord
Randolph (who was staying at Windsor) thereupon
(December 20) wrote to the Prime Minister a letter
of resignation. It is sufficient to quote from it a
couple of sentences:

I know that on this subject I cannot look for any
sympathy or effective support from you, and I am
certain that I shall find no supporters in the Cabinet.
I do not want to be wrangling and quarrelling in the
Cabinet, and therefore must request to be allowed to
give up my office and retire from the Government.

Lord Salisbury does not seem to have communicated this letter to the Queen, and it was not for
two days that he sent a reply (December 22) which,
while expressing " profound regret ", was a definite
acceptance of the resignation. Lord Randolph treated
it as such, as appears from his rejoinder of the day,
of which the concluding paragraph is as follows:

The character of the domestic legislation which
the Government contemplate in my opinion falls
sadly short of what Parliament and the country expect and require. The foreign policy which is being
adopted appears to me at once dangerous and
methodless; but I take my stand on expenditure and
finance, which involve and determine all other mat-

ters. And reviewing my former public declarations on this question, and having no reason to doubt their soundness, I take leave of your Government, and especially of yourself, with profound regret, but without doubt or hesitation.

As soon as this letter was written, Lord Randolph went to the office of the *Times,* and told the editor exactly the state of the case, with the result that the first announcement of the startling *coup de théâtre* appeared in the issue of that newspaper on the morning of the twenty-third. It was also the first intimation that the Queen had had of what had been going on.

The exact motives of Lord Randolph's resignation will always be a matter of speculation. That he played his cards as badly as the most bungling amateur could have done, is, of course, clear beyond doubt. The simplest explanation is the most probable. He did not believe that, when it came to the point, his resignation would be accepted. He was convinced that he had become the *homme nécessaire.* It was inconceivable to him that he should be jettisoned in preference to the Smiths and the Hamiltons. Lord G. Hamilton (in his " Parliamentary Reminiscences ") puts it down to a " sudden and ungovernable impulse " due to excessive strain which had unbalanced the nervous system.[7] I see nothing in the circumstances to justify this pathological hypothesis. As Mr. Churchill says, he had given the Cab-

---

[7] " Parliamentary Reminiscences and Reflections ", 1886–1906; pp. 51–52.

inet " long and ample notice of his intention. He
reiterated his determination at intervals through the
autumn." In a conversation (already referred to)
which I had with him years afterwards (1891), and
which I recorded at the time, he said to me: " When
I resigned I should have beaten Lord Salisbury, as *I
confidently expected to do,* but for their being able
to fall back on Goschen." He added: " If I had
beaten, there would have been no coercion, an Irish
Local Government Bill, and a ' truly Liberal ' policy
like that of '68–'74."

It was not an " ungovernable impulse ", but faulty
calculation, which was his undoing.

There is no more dramatic incident in the political
history of our time than the sudden downfall of
Randolph Churchill. For downfall it was — complete
and irretrievable. It may almost be said that from
that moment he, who had carried everything before
him and was still under forty, though in the few
years which still remained to him of life there was
now and again a spasmodic eruption of the old fires,
ceased to count as an effective political force.

CHAPTER XXVII

RESHUFFLING THE PACK, 1887

THE resignation of Lord Randolph Churchill was a blow to the Salisbury Government under which, for the moment, it reeled to its very foundations. Its one member (apart from the Prime Minister) who combined brilliant talent with popular authority had disappeared. The rest, with one or two exceptions, who had yet to prove their capacity — and leaving on one side Sir M. Hicks Beach, stricken with a physical disability which almost immediately compelled his retirement — were, to tell the naked truth, a drab-coloured team of more or less experienced mediocrities. There was no one in the whole Tory Party, whether inside or outside the Administration, who had any title or any qualifications to step into Lord Randolph's place. So far, his calculations had been well-founded.

Lord Salisbury was, therefore, confronted with a most embarrassing problem. He had one fixed resolve: that no power — Olympian, Terrestrial, or Tartarean — should ever induce him to go again into active partnership with the versatile and unmanageable colleague whom he had just lost. In his perplexity he turned to Lord Hartington, who was

" studying antiquities " at Rome, and implored him
to return without delay. Lord Hartington, who, no
doubt, suspected the purpose for which he was
wanted, was in no hurry, and broke his journey at
Monte Carlo, where he found a letter from Lord
Salisbury with a proposal that he should either form
a Coalition Government, or join the existing Government as Leader of the House of Commons. The
Queen wrote to him on Christmas Day, earnestly and
whole-heartedly backing Lord Salisbury's offer.

Thus, for the third time, the highest office under
the Crown was put at Lord Hartington's disposal.
For the third time he refused it; probably a unique
experience in the career of a British statesman.[1] His
reasons — among which he gives a prominent place
to the obvious fact that his appointment as head

---

[1] It is worth while recording here Sir W. Harcourt's opinion of Lord
Hartington (in a letter to Morley, December 30, 1891): " Nothing I
think is more obvious than that Hartington is destined to be at the head
of affairs as soon as we go out, which will be about six weeks after we
go in. I myself have a great public respect as well as personal regard for
the man. He has immense advantage — so rare in this *fin de siècle* —
of having no d——d nonsense about him. He is almost worthy to have
lived in the eighteenth century." (" Gardiner ", II, 156.) This was the
highest compliment that Sir William could pay. He wrote to Mr. Morley
when he was at work on his monograph on Walpole: " I am glad to
know you are doing Walpole, though I fear you are not worthy of him.
I doubt if your philosophical and casuist spirit can really sympathize
with his fine and brutal antagonism to damned nonsense, which is sometimes called the ' spirit of the Age.' . . . I am a thorough eighteenth
century man in disposition, education, sentiment and connexion . . . I
once told (Mr. G.) that I thought W. the greatest minister who ever
ruled in England. He did not like it. It is all nonsense about his corrup-
tion. He paid the fools to do what the wise men told them — a very good
bargain. After all, it was the Philistines who made England, just as the
idéologues ruined France. They are, however, perishing so fast under the
jawbones of asses, that I fear there is little left for us in the future."
(*Ibid.*, 142–143.)

of the Government would have been unpalatable
and even obnoxious to the rank and file of the
Conservative Party — are stated with his usual
clearness and force in his letter (December 31) to
the Queen.[2]

To the alternative suggestion — that he and some
of his friends should join the existing Government —
he gave a still more emphatic negative. " Such a
course would," he said, " inevitably bring about the
dissolution of the Liberal Unionist Party." This
opinion, however, did not prevent him from using all
his influence to persuade Mr. Goschen to accept Lord
Salisbury's offer of the Exchequer. Goschen was supposed to stand in a different category from the other
Liberal Unionist leaders, for the strange reason that
his views on the franchise had prevented him from
being a member of the Gladstone Administration of
1880 to 1885. After some hesitations, and apparently
with many doubts, he at last yielded to Lord Hartington's pressure, with the stipulation that he was to
be free to state that in joining Lord Salisbury's Government " he had not become a Conservative, or
ceased to hold any of his Liberal opinions."

Accordingly Mr. Goschen took Lord Randolph's
place at the Exchequer. It was sought to mitigate
his solitude in the Cabinet by finding one or two
Liberal Unionist peers to accompany him, but the
search was unavailing. For the next five years —
indeed, until the death of the Salisbury Government
— he remained its only Liberal Unionist member,

[2] It is set out in " Devonshire ", II, 179–181.

and became the chosen target for the gibes and sarcasms of the more ardent and aggressive spirits in
the Liberal Opposition.[3] He was, despite a raucous
voice and some uncouth tricks of gesture, an admirable debater, with a style and a method entirely his
own, and he always gave as good as he got.

There still remained the question of the leadership
of the House, which Mr. Goschen in the circumstances naturally refused to undertake. As if to
advertise in the most dramatic way that he was making a new departure, Lord Salisbury confided this
part of Lord Randolph's double functions to Mr. W.
H. Smith, with the office of First Lord of the Treasury. Mr. Smith had been one of Lord Randolph's
favourite butts in his salad days, as a partner in the
legendary political firm of " Marshall and Snel-
grove " ; and his contrast between the " pineries and
vineries " of the opulent bourgeois and his own
" humble roof " — whatever may be thought of its
taste — was one of his happiest and most effective
sallies.[4] Mr. Smith is one of those men whose rise to
high power in the State is as difficult to account for
as it is creditable to themselves and to their country.
He had spent his youth and early middle age in building up, almost literally with his own hands, and by
none but the most honourable means, an immense
business which supplied an urgent and growing public
need, and which yielded him an ample fortune. He
belonged by birth and association to the middle class

[3] The " Broker's man in possession " was the subject of one of
Frank Lockwood's best caricatures.   [4] *See ante,* p. 125.

(largely Nonconformist) which dominated English politics from 1832 to 1868. That class had been for more than the lifetime of a generation the backbone of the Liberal Party in the country; and one of the early signs of a new orientation is to be seen in the fact that it was as a Conservative and a Churchman that Smith sought to enter Parliament for the City of Westminster, where he defeated no less eminent an antagonist than J. S. Mill at the general election of 1868.

He became a useful and assiduous Member, with no pretensions of any kind to debating skill, and had the reputation of a sound, solid, genial man, when Mr. Disraeli (who had a seeing eye and no prejudice) picked him out for office, and ultimately gave him a place in his Cabinet. He then took his place as a regular member of what the Fourth Party used to call the " Old Gang ", and the bodyguard of the " Goat "; and, though he was of little or no use as a speaker, he carried weight with his colleagues, and was even chosen as the " Emergency Man " who was sent to Dublin in search of an Irish policy in January, 1886.

Such was Lord Randolph's successor in the leadership of the House. And such he remained to the end — four years later — when he succumbed under the double burden of excessive labour and failing health. If he left no footprint in the history of Parliament, no man ever tried harder, or with more universal esteem and good will — in his own favourite phrase — to do his " duty to his Queen and country."

We must at this point bid farewell to another figure, which had been for more than a generation in the forefront of the political stage, and at one time (as has been seen) seemed to be cast for the leading part. Sir Stafford Northcote, when his leadership of the House of Commons in the first Salisbury Administration in 1885 had been in effect vetoed by Lord R. Churchill, was created an Earl and given a sinecure office in the Cabinet.[5] In the second Salisbury Administration of July, 1886, Lord Iddesleigh (as he was now called) received the Foreign Office, where, as has been already shown, his policy was, during the autumn, the subject of a good deal of malevolent criticism from Lord R. Churchill. Lord Salisbury now resolved, taking advantage of Lord Iddesleigh's offer (usual when a Government is being reconstructed) to put the office at his disposal, to resume it himself. There seems to have been a regrettable want of tact in the way in which the transaction was handled, and Lord Iddesleigh declined the compensation offered him of the presidency of the Council. On January 12, 1887, he walked across from the Foreign Office to Number 10, Downing Street, to say farewell to the Prime Minister, was seized with a heart attack, and died in the presence of Lord Salisbury.

Lord R. Churchill wrote the next day to Lord Salisbury a letter of condolence, in which with a faint twinge of compunction, he says, " I felt much the old Lord's death, for he had for years past gone through much bother, disappointment and probably vexation,

[5] *See ante*, p. 132.

nor can I conveniently repress the reflection *quorum pars magna fui.*"

Lord Salisbury's reply reveals the capacity for deep and genuine emotion which he rarely betrayed to outsiders:

> I had never happened to see anyone die before, and, therefore, even apart from the circumstances, the suddenness of this unexpected death would have been shocking. But here was, in addition, the thought of our thirty years' companionship in political life; and the reflection that now, just before this sudden parting, by some strange misunderstanding which it is hopeless to explain, I had I believe for the first time in my life, seriously wounded his feelings. As I looked upon the dead body stretched before me, I felt that politics was a cursed profession.[6]

6 " Churchill ", pp. 651–652.

CHAPTER XXVIII

THE House of Commons, elected in the summer of 1886, was not dissolved until the summer of 1892. Its main achievement in the sphere of domestic legislation was the passing of two Local Government Acts, for England and Wales, and for Scotland, which were conceived in the main on democratic lines, apart from some incidental provisions, such as the proposal to create a vested interest in annual liquor licences, which was dropped largely in consequence of the determined efforts of Sir William Harcourt. There was no longer any talk or thought on the Government side of the " *great signposts of our policy* [1] — equality, similarity and simultaneity — in the development of a genuinely popular system of government in all the four countries which form the United Kingdom."

None the less, it was the fourth country which dominated, and, to a large extent, absorbed the time and the controversial energies of this Parliament during the whole of its life.

It is not necessary to waste many sentences over the " Round Table Conference " held in January,

---

[1] *See ante,* p. 172.

1887, between certain of the Liberal and Liberal Unionist leaders, with the ostensible object of discovering an Eirenicon on Irish policy. Mr. Chamberlain, who seems to have been genuinely alarmed for the moment at the withdrawal, through Lord R. Churchill's resignation, of the only Liberal influence in the Government, started the idea in a speech at Birmingham, which held out at once a signal of distress and a flag of truce. Mr. Gladstone and Lord Hartington took no direct part in the confabulations which followed, though the former, at any rate, regarded them with tempered benignity. The whole story is graphically and impartially told in Mr. Gardiner's " Life of Harcourt." It was really a grotesque affair. The method of procedure adopted was such that it did not prevent the members of the Conference, or some of them, from leaving the privacy of the Round Table from time to time for the platform, and saying in public candid and unpalatable things. The climax was reached when Mr. Chamberlain wrote a letter to a Welsh correspondent, published in a Nonconformist newspaper, the *Baptist,* than which nothing could have been better calculated to exasperate his Gladstonian colleagues. It contained the following passage:

Thirty-two millions of people must go without much-needed legislation because three millions are disloyal, while nearly six hundred members of the Imperial Parliament will be reduced to forced inactivity because some eighty delegates representing the policy and receiving the pay of the Chicago Convention, are determined to obstruct all business until their demands have been conceded.

After this the Conference never met again. The severance between Mr. Chamberlain and the bulk of the Liberal Party was from that time definite; and in the following session his association with and active support of the Government policy of coercion, made the gulf month by month wider and deeper, and in the end impassable.

The session of 1887 was the most arduous in my recollection, or I suppose in that of any of my contemporaries. There was no limitation to the length of our sittings; indeed, it was calculated that during the session the House sat 277 hours after midnight, and not infrequently it did not rise till three or four in the morning. For those who, like myself and probably a majority of the members, were busily engaged in their own affairs during the day, the strain was such as only youth, or an ironclad constitution, could withstand. Mr. W. H. Smith, the Leader of the House, was no longer a young man, but always stuck gallantly to his post, and I imagine never really recovered from the ordeal of this year.[2]

The real trouble in Ireland at this time was not so much political as agrarian. No impartial student can doubt that, notwithstanding the sporadic reductions made by the Land Courts under the Act of 1881, rents over a large part of the country were still in excess of what the tenants could pay; the burden of

[2] It was one of the hottest summers ever known, and time and energy had to be found for the official junketings of the First Jubilee.

arrears was always accumulating; and the landlords and their agents were resorting freely to the power of eviction. Hicks Beach, in these circumstances, was, in Lord R. Churchill's words, " afraid of being forced to administer Ireland too much on a landlords' rights basis ",[3] and he was accused of exercising a " dispensing power " in the giving or withholding of police protection when landlords were resorting to their remedy. This he denied, but it was not disputed that he had called in to his aid a distinguished soldier, Sir Redvers Buller, with the status of a divisional magistrate, and with instructions that he and other magistrates should, in the case of threatened evictions, use all the influence in their power to promote a settlement. A Bill by Parnell to deal with the situation had been rejected in the autumn session of 1886. Early in the New Year the people took matters into their own hands, and organized, under the leadership of Mr. John Dillon and Mr. William O'Brien (without the approval of Mr. Parnell) the plan of campaign, under which the tenants of an estate proffered what they had agreed among themselves to be a reasonable rent, and if it was not accepted as payment in full, handed over the money to a committee to be used for the purposes of the struggle.

Things had reached this pass, when Sir M. Hicks Beach threatened (as he was advised) with blindness, felt compelled to resign, and was succeeded in the office of Chief Secretary by Mr. A. J. Balfour.

Mr. Balfour had at this time been thirteen years

[3] " Churchill ", p. 603.

in the House; he had taken a fitful, though not an inactive, part in the guerilla campaigns of the Fourth Party; he had recently been admitted to a place in the Cabinet; but it cannot be said that he was as yet a commanding parliamentary figure. He was known to be a man of great intellectual distinction, much admired and sought after in society; but he was thought to sit rather loosely by politics; to be unconsumed, if not unsinged, by the fires of ambition; and to be the last man who would aspire to the drudgeries and the hazards of the most exacting and unattractive post in the Government. Few have more rapidly or more completely falsified the expectations both of their friendly and their hostile critics. Perhaps as good an illustration as any of the changed light in which he came soon to be regarded, is to be found in the flexible vocabulary of Nationalist invective, where, having started as a " Tiger Lily ", and the "pampered Darling of a perfumed drawing-room ", he developed into a " Plaster of Paris Cromwell ", and finished up as the " base, bloody and brutal Balfour."

Whether or not Sir M. Hicks Beach had assented, before his retirement, to the initiation of a policy of coercion, *sans phrase,* there is, so far as I know, no authentic evidence, one way or the other, yet given to the world. But his successor did not leave a moment's doubt as to his own intentions, which must, of course, have been ratified by the Cabinet. His first step was to introduce the Bill — afterwards known as the Crimes Act — which from its parliamentary inception, and through all the succeeding years of his administration, was the central point of the political battlefield.

There were, undoubtedly, grave features, from the point of view of law and order, in the social conditions of Ireland; the most serious being the prevalence of organized boycotting, and the indisposition of juries to convict, even upon overwhelming evidence, where the crime charged against the accused had an agrarian complexion. There was on the Statute Book, in the way of precedent, a plentiful array of so-called Coercion Acts, some of them, such as that of 1882, of Gladstonian parentage. Mr. Balfour's Bill, however, contained two new features: (1) Unlike all its predecessors, it had no limit in its duration; it stigmatized Ireland, as Mr. Gladstone contended, with a " permanent brand of inferiority "; (2) it substituted for a jury, the summary jurisdiction of two resident magistrates (removable at the discretion of the Executive) in the case of a number of indictable offences, of which the most practically important were criminal conspiracy, riot, unlawful assembly, and incitement to any of them.

Over this Bill, in all its stages in the House of Commons and, after it became an Act, in all the successive phases of its administration in Ireland, there raged the sharpest and most embittered controversy of our time. In Parliament the remodelled Closure was constantly resorted to by the Government, and it was to secure the passage of this measure that the instrument, afterwards known as the " Guil-

lotine ", was invented and freely applied by Mr.
Smith and his colleagues. The Liberal Unionists,
many of them with unconcealed reluctance, supported
it throughout. One of the most significant tests of
their new allegiance was afforded at the very outset,
when the Government proposed, in order to further
the progress of the Bill, to take the whole time of the
House. It so happened that the first motion on the
paper, which this procedure would set aside, was one
relating to the Welsh Church. Mr. Bright was present, and Lord George Hamilton records in his " Reminiscences " [4] that he watched how the author of the
dictum that " Force is no remedy " and the Apostle
of disestablishment, would face this searching ordeal.
The division bell rang, and Bright, " carrying his
leonine head with more assertiveness than usual ",
rose from his seat immediately behind Mr. Gladstone
and walked into the Government lobby. Chamberlain, though the ink of his letter to the *Baptist* was
hardly yet dry, followed in his steps. The third reading of the Bill was supported by Hartington, Bright,
Chamberlain, Sir H. James and Courtney. Sir G.
Trevelyan had now definitely broken with his new
allies, and had been returned as a Gladstonian at
a by-election in Glasgow. He was sneered at by
Chamberlain as a " perfect specimen of a political
weather-cock ", and likened by Mr. Balfour to Mr.
Pliable in the " Pilgrim's Progress."

The only occasion on which the loyalty of the

[4] " Parliamentary Reminiscences and Reflections ", 1886–1906, pp.
65–66.

Liberal Unionists to their new friends was strained
to breaking point was when the National League was
proclaimed under the old Act as a " dangerous Association." Even Hartington professed to Ministers his
serious doubts, and Chamberlain, after strongly re-
monstrating with them in private, went so far as to
vote in the division lobby for Mr. Gladstone's motion
of condemnation. It was about this time that Lord
Randolph took occasion to describe them as a " useful
kind of crutch to the Government."

The administration of the new law gave rise to
as much bitter criticism as its enactment. " Remember Mitchelstown " became a watchword with Liberals as well as with Nationalists, who were now to
be seen speaking on the same platforms in Great
Britain, and it is no exaggeration to say that the
rank and file of the Liberal Unionists in the country,
profoundly alienated by Mr. Balfour's reactionary
methods, were, in the years 1888 to 1890, in thousands rejoining their old party. By the beginning of
1889 the Chief Secretary had under lock and key
some twenty-five Nationalist members of the House
of Commons.

I may be allowed to cite, not for any special merits
of its own, but as a concise and handy summary of
the Liberal indictment of the Balfour régime, a
speech which I made in the House of Commons on
March 1, 1889:

" Coercion has hitherto been regarded by English
statesmen as a disagreeable duty, imposed perhaps by
necessity, but to be accepted with reluctance, and

exercised with temper, dignity and tact. The right honourable gentleman has changed all that. He resented the other night, with much indignation, charges of cynicism and brutality. I am not fond of using abusive epithets; but I am persuaded that neither the right honourable gentleman nor any of his colleagues even now realize the deep-seated and widespread sentiment of repugnance which his methods of administration have inspired. . . . The right honourable gentleman was entrusted by Parliament with special powers for a special purpose. And what was that purpose? It was to put down crime. How has he used those powers? He has directed the main brunt of his prosecutions, not against moonlighters and outrage-mongers, but against some of the most blameless and universally-respected of his political opponents. He has had them arrested at times and in places which seem to have been deliberately selected for the purpose of inflicting wanton indignity, and, at any rate, of suggesting to the minds of the people of Great Britain that the action of the Executive was dictated by political vindictiveness. He has had them tried on charges, in support of which the vague and elastic law of conspiracy has been tortured to purposes for which it was never intended, and to which I do not hesitate to say in this country it never has been, and I trust to Heaven it never will be, applied. He has constituted for their trial, tribunals of which I say, deliberately, speaking with a full sense of responsibility and having carefully watched their proceedings, that in the short space of two years they have brought ridicule and contempt on the name of law in Ireland. And then, Sir, after sentence, when he has got them into prison, he has subjected them — men, by his own admission, mistaken and misguided, if you please, but still the victims of a genuine, if perverted, enthusiasm — to the lot of the commonest felons, declining to exercise in their favour the power of relaxation expressly given to him by statute, and which he himself used in a particular class of cases. While these things have been going on in Ireland, what has the right honourable gentleman himself been doing? So far as the public are able to know, he has divided his time between making rollicking and roystering speeches, in which he has sharpened a very pretty wit on the alleged absurdities of men who could not reply to him, and writing or dictating letters which I venture to think will serve as models for all time of smart and flippant inaccuracy."

CHAPTER XXIX

PIGOTT, 1888–1889

ANOTHER circumstance which, between 1888 and 1890, did almost as much as the scandals of Coercion to swell the tide now setting strongly in favour of Home Rule, was the institution and the proceedings of what was known as the Parnell Commission. The *Times* which, with the object of discrediting the Nationalists, had been publishing a series of articles under the title " Parnellism and Crime ", on the morning of the division on the second reading of the Crimes Bill, circulated (April, 1887) the facsimile of a letter, which purported to be signed by Parnell himself, in effect condoning the Phœnix Park murders. Parnell rose in his place the same evening in the House of Commons immediately before the division, and described the document as a villainous and bare-faced forgery. Later on in the year a Mr. O'Donnell, who had been a Nationalist member, brought an action for libel against the *Times* on the ground that he was one of the persons affected by their imputations. At the trial before the Lord Chief Justice in July, 1888, the Judge held that the plaintiff had not made out any case of libel against himself. Sir R. Webster, the Attorney-General, who appeared for the *Times,* nevertheless succeeded in making a speech which lasted three days, and in the course of which he produced other alleged letters which " carried complicity and connivance with crime to a further point ", but he made no attempt (on the ground that it was not necessary for the purposes of the trial) to prove their genuineness. Parnell lost no time in denouncing the new letters as also forgeries, and asked for a Select Committee of the House to inquire into their authenticity. This was refused by the Government, who offered in exchange a Statutory Commission of three Judges to inquire generally into the charges and allegations made in the *Times* articles against Members of Parliament and " other persons."

This proposal, which was manifestly unfair in its extension of the field of inquiry, and singularly ill-conceived in the unfitness of the proposed tribunal for the determination of such matters as were to be submitted to it, was embodied in a Bill which was carried through by a liberal use of the closure and guillotine. The Opposition sought in vain to confine the issue to be decided to the authenticity of the letters.

Lord R. Churchill hotly disapproved of the proposed procedure, and though he held his tongue in the House, he drew up and submitted to Mr. Smith an admirable and closely-reasoned Memorandum of protest which concludes with these words: " I do not examine the party aspects of the matter: I only remark that the fate of the Union may be determined by the abnormal proceedings of an abnormal tri-

bunal. Prudent politicians would hesitate to go out of
their way to play such high stakes as these." [1]

The Commission was duly set up in the autumn of
1888; it sat on one hundred twenty-nine days, and
examined some five hundred witnesses.

Sir Charles Russell and I were Mr. Parnell's
counsel, and in the whole of my forensic life I have
never been engaged in any proceeding which could
compare with this for sustained dreariness and futile
waste of time, lit up, on perhaps five or six days out
of the one hundred twenty-nine with scenes of
poignant and unforgettable drama. Russell and I
knew from the first that the letters were forgeries,
and by whom they had been forged. But months
were squandered over obscure incidents in Cork and
Kerry and Galway, and a long procession of district
inspectors and resident magistrates, together with at
least one professional spy, were put into the box to
prove the thesis that " Crime dogged the footsteps of
the League ", before the Court was allowed to approach the only issue which had led to its appointment, or upon which the world cared anything for its
judgment. That moment at last came; the demonstration of the truth was irresistible and even easy;
and when the wretched Pigott fled and took his life,
the vindication of Parnell was complete.

The report of the Commission was not made until
February, 1890; it covered a lot of ground and excited little interest. It was the subject of an animated
debate in the House in March, which is only memo-

[1] The Memorandum is printed at length in " Churchill ", pp. 757–760.

rable now for two speeches, those of Lord R. Churchill (the last, I think, in which he approached his old self) and of Mr. Gladstone. I give brief citations from both:

Lord R. Churchill: The procedure which we are called upon to stamp with our approval to-night is a procedure which would undoubtedly have been gladly resorted to by the Tudors and their judges. It is procedure of an arbitrary and tyrannical character used against individuals who are political opponents of the Government of the day — procedure such as Parliament has for generations and centuries struggled against and resisted — procedure such as we had hoped, in these happy days, Parliament had triumphantly overcome. It is procedure such as would have startled even Lord Eldon; it is procedure such as Lords Lyndhurst and Brougham would have protested against; it is procedure which if the great lawyer Earl Cairns had been alive, the Tory Party would never have carried. But a Nemesis awaits a Government that adopts unconstitutional methods. What has been the result of this uprootal of constitutional practice? What has been the one result? Pigott! — a man, a thing, a reptile, a monster — Pigott! Pigott! Pigott!

Mr. Gladstone: And now, Sir, as a member of the minority, to whom am I to appeal? I appeal from the party opposite to the party opposite. I appeal from them as a party to them as individuals. I ask you as citizens — I will not say as Christians — and as men, to consider this case. I ask you to acknowledge the law of equal and reciprocal moral obligation; I ask you to place yourselves for a moment —

not the mass among whom responsibility is diffused
and severed till it becomes inoperative and worthless,
but I ask you individually, man by man, to place
yourselves in the position of the Honourable Member
for Cork as the victim of this frightful outrage. Is it
possible, in doing this, after all his cares, all his suffering, all that he has gone through — and I believe
there is no parallel to it at least for two hundred
years — that you can fail to feel that something remains due to him, or that you can bring that something lower or make it smaller than I have put it in
the amendment? No, Sir. Then give, I pray you to
give, give it as men, but do not be satisfied with giving a judgment that may be sustained by the cheers
of a majority of this House upon a victorious or favourable decision, give such a judgment as will bear
the scrutiny of the heart and of the conscience of
every man when he takes himself to his chamber and
is still. Of such a judgment I have no fear. For such
a judgment, I ask you, I entreat you, I urge you, I
might almost say, in the name of that law of reciprocal obligation, I respectfully demand it of you. Give
such a judgment in the terms of the amendment, concur in declaring that which is, after all, but a part,
and a feebly drawn and represented part, of the
wrongs that have been inflicted — give that judgment, accede to our demand, accede to our prayer,
and grant this late, this measured, this perhaps
scanty, reparation of an enormous and unheard-of
wrong.

CHAPTER XXX

PARNELL, 1890

THE effect of the Pigott exposure was enormous. It might be true (as Lord Salisbury characteristically observed) that " the fact that a Nationalist journalist had forged the signature of a Nationalist leader was no proof that the latter possessed every statesman-like quality and virtue." But the personal vindication of Parnell, now proved to have been a much wronged man, who, confronted with a vile charge, had shown both manly indignation and dignified patience, was in itself a great asset to the Nationalist cause. It aroused the kind of sympathy which is best worth having, and which is always potentially present in the British character — the sympathy which springs not from sentimentalism, but from an outraged sense of fair play. It predisposed the average man, who had not sworn allegiance to any party, to be suspicious and even sceptical when the itinerant orators of the " Loyal and Patriotic Union ", from Ulster and elsewhere, went on repeating that Home Rule would mean the joint ascendancy of the Pope and Captain Moonlight. Nor did some of the Unionist leaders escape a share of the odium which covered the unhappy manager of the *Times*. They had shown themselves almost as gullible as poor Simon Macdonald himself.

The stars seemed at last to be fighting in their courses for Home Rule. The growing discredit of Balfourism, and the triumphant exoneration of Parnell, had unquestionably not a little to do with the steady success of the Liberal candidates in the by-elections. In the late autumn of 1890, as Lord Morley notes in his " Recollections ", " the quicksilver stood delightfully high in our barometer."

It is to be remembered that the verdict of the country when Mr. Gladstone appealed to it in 1886 had been by no means of a decisive character. The idea of Home Rule as a practical policy, to be embodied in immediate legislation, was then still new and strange to the electorate. It was, moreover (as has already been pointed out) a grievous handicap to the first Home Rule Bill that at the general election it had to be run in double harness with a Land Bill for which nobody had a good word to say. Much the most effective of the electoral placards in that contest were those which depicted trainloads of trucks with golden sovereigns which had been extracted from the pockets of the British taxpayer, and were consigned to the Irish landlords. Notwithstanding these drawbacks, in the total poll 1,344,000 voted for Mr. Gladstone's policy, and 1,420,000 (Conservatives 1,041,000, Liberal Unionists 379,000) voted against it. The Gladstonian poll in the contested constituencies thus largely exceeded the Conservative, and was only 76,000 behind Conservative and Liberal Unionist combined.[1]

[1] Morley, " Gladstone ", III, 346.

It is not, therefore, a matter for surprise that in the summer of 1890 the political prophets predicted a substantial Home Rule majority in Great Britain (apart from Ireland) at the general election which could not be long delayed. Sanguine Liberals (including Mr. Gladstone himself) looked for a " three-figure " majority.

The bottom was knocked out of these calculations when, on November 17, 1890, Captain O'Shea obtained a decree of divorce against his wife in a suit to which Mr. Parnell was co-respondent.

The story of what followed; of Mr. Gladstone's reluctant but inevitable intervention; of Parnell's charges of intended perfidy and treachery against the Liberal leader; of his ultimate repudiation by the bulk of his parliamentary following; of his desperate struggle against overwhelming odds to regain his foothold in Ireland; of the sudden change from the frigid and rhetoric, at once impassive and impressive, to which the House of Commons was accustomed, to the writhings and curses of a baffled and half-demented Titan; until the end overtook the still defiant and undefeated spirit in October, 1891; all this has been depicted by one who was a first-hand witness, in perhaps the most dramatic pages of Lord Morley's biography.

> " The little dogs and all
> Tray, Blanch and Sweetheart,"

who had fed out of his hand, were in full cry, hounding him to his doom. It may be said that he deserved

it. Had he not betrayed their fidelity, flouted their
devotion, done his worst in the most squalid and ignoble fashion to ruin their cause, and that of their
and his country? All the same, it was a sorry and
indeed a tragic spectacle. I shocked some of my excellent friends at the time by avowing that, if I had
been an Irish Nationalist member I should have been
more than tempted to be also a Parnellite. I will
quote from Lord Morley's narrative only a single
passage for the light which it throws upon Mr. Gladstone's attitude from the first:

Mr. Gladstone always steadfastly resisted every
call to express an opinion of his own that the delin-
quency itself had made Mr. Parnell unfit and impossible. . . . He adhered tenaciously to political
ground. " I have been for four years," he argued,
" endeavouring to persuade voters to support Irish
autonomy. Now the voter says to me: ' If a certain
thing happens — namely, the retention of the leadership in its present hands — I will not support Irish
autonomy.' How can I go on with the work? We
laboriously rolled the great stone up to the top of the
hill, and now it topples down to the bottom again,
unless Mr. Parnell sees fit to go." [2]

There can be little doubt that a decisive factor in
the turn of events was Mr. Gladstone's intimation in
his letter to Mr. Morley, that the " continuance at
the present moment of (Parnell) in the leadership
would render my retention of the leadership of the
Liberal Party, based as it has been mainly upon the
prosecution of the Irish cause, almost a nullity."

[2] Morley, " Gladstone ", III, 435.

Mr. John Redmond, who was one of the few who adhered to Parnell to the end, said in the course of the heated debates in Committee Room 15, that " in selling our leader to preserve the Liberal alliance, we are selling the independence of the Irish Party." This became the Parnellite keynote. " Save me," said Parnell in one of his frantic appeals to the Irish people, " from the English wolves now howling for my destruction." But it was of no avail.

Parnell's character and career are, and are likely to remain, one of the unsolved enigmas of history. It has often been said that there is no other instance of a man with so few popular gifts enlisting so rapidly and so completely the devoted following of a people. He was not only not a demagogue; he was not, and never pretended to be, a democrat. His ascendancy over his parliamentary colleagues (some of them men of conspicuous faculty) was equally unquestioned; and survived, unimpaired, his habitual and almost ostentatious indifference both to their counsels and their convenience; his complete isolation from them except on the platform or the floor of the House; and the wayward irregularities of his life, which made it impossible to forecast his views, or even to count upon his attendance, in the most critical emergencies of the parliamentary game. He seemed at times to take a grim and freakish pleasure in straining their allegiance almost to the breaking point. It was not till his criminal selfishness jeopardized the whole fortunes of their common cause that he heard for the

Photograph by Lawrence of Dublin

CHARLES STEWART PARNELL

first time more than a whisper of remonstrance, still less was confronted by a gesture of mutiny.

I had more opportunities than most Englishmen of studying him at close quarters, for during the best part of a year (when the Commission was sitting) I used to see him almost daily; certainly three or four times a week. He would come to my chambers in the Temple, and sit there *tête-à-tête* for an hour or more at a time. Ostensibly our business was to discuss and to provide in advance against the shifting and often unexpected phases of the case. But we often digressed to other matters, and though he was by nature the most reticent and reserved of men, he would sometimes expose, for a few moments at any rate, something of what lay beneath the frost-bound and unresponsive surface.

He had been an undergraduate at Cambridge, and played cricket in his College Eleven, but so far as I could ever discover, he was almost without a tincture of literature. Such interests of an intellectual kind as he had were in the domain, perhaps the outskirts of the domain, of science, and I gathered that he spent a good many odd hours doing experiments in a laboratory. He was not well read even in Irish history. In the heyday of the " union of hearts " I was one of a small dinner party at Mr. Armitstead's, the chief guests being Mr. Gladstone and Mr. Parnell, who, I think, were meeting in private for the first time. I can still remember the pained and puzzled look which came over my venerable Leader's face when the Irishman betrayed complete ignorance of

the date and purpose of Lord Fitzwilliam's mission
to Dublin. Nor had Parnell any natural gift of expression. I never heard him say what is called a good
thing, and one can search his speeches in vain for a
picturesque or even an arresting phrase. I can best
describe the general impression which our colloquies
left upon me, as that of a man whose mind was
a strange compound of insight and obtuseness; one
might almost say of genius and stupidity; who saw
at intervals things which other people did not see;
but who was apt to be inconceivably blind to things
which almost everybody else saw.

I will give a single illustration drawn from the
proceedings of the Commission.

Towards the close of the inquiry, after the exposure of the forged letters, and when all public
interest in the affair was languishing, Parnell was put
into the box. Sir R. Webster's cross-examination,
which lasted many days, was a monumental exhi-
bition of forensic futility; but late on a Friday afternoon, when every one's powers of endurance (including Parnell's) were all but exhausted, Sir Richard
cited a passage from some speech of his in Parliament
which Parnell found it difficult at the moment to
jusify or even to explain. " Do you mean, Mr. Parnell," asked Counsel in his most solemn tones, " that
you intended to deceive the House of Commons? "
Parnell replied with weary *insouciance,* " I suppose
I did."

As we walked away from the court to our usual
consultation, Parnell (who was, as I have said, an old

cricketer) remarked to me with unruffled compla-
cency, " Didn't you think Webster's bowling very
wide to-day? " " The bowling was wide enough," I
growled, " if you hadn't hit your wicket."

A week or so before the final crash, I met him in
the Temple on his way to see his Counsel in the
Divorce Case, in which I was not engaged.

He was more alert and debonnair than was his
wont, and I said to him: " Well — is it going to be all
right? " He smiled almost genially and replied, " Of
course it is! You needn't worry about that." The
truth is that he had a marvellous faculty of self-
deception, and I feel sure that he believed that after
nine days of gossip the whole thing would blow over
and be forgotten. There can, I think, be little doubt
that in him, as in his highly gifted sister Fanny, there
was a morbid streak which, in time, affected both
brain and will.

But the Irish Party never recovered his loss.

NOTE [3]

1891. October 16: A couple of hours with John
Morley. . . . At the end of 1886 Parnell came to
see J. M. to ask his opinion about the Plan of Campaign. M. said its effect upon British electors would
be bad; they would think it immoral, etc. P. said
that it would have a still worse result — that it would
afford a pretext for Coercion which would be bad
both for the Plan and for the whole movement. (This

[3] I kept a diary for about two years, from 1891 to 1893. The following note is an extract from the entry of October 16, 1891 — ten days
after Parnell's death.

was what afterwards happened.) I told J. M. about
P.'s statement to me (about September, 1888) that
it was a mistake to suppose that Coercion would be
futile;[4] the Irish could not stand it, and (if it was
steadfastly applied) would yield to it: his object had
always been not to fight but to prevent Coercion.

J. M. first met P. at a dinner given at Richmond
in 1877 by J. Chamberlain. He had then invented
obstruction, and was fighting flogging in the Army,
etc. Even then John Bright would not speak to him.
P. drove back to London with them and sat on the
box; he was then young and very handsome — like a
Meredith hero.

We talked of his character. Mr. G. is all for for-
getting the last ten months and ranks him with Grat-
tan and O'Connell. M. thinks his estimate too high:
something *mesquin* in his character. I, on the other
hand, contended that, looking at him as a force in
the world, it was too low: that judging by results,
clearly traceable to one man's initiative, by the dead-
heave given, he was one of the three or four men of
the century. M. was inclined to agree. He thought
P. deteriorated and was almost fatuous in the months
before the Commission, when he vacillated about
bringing an action, etc., but this was due to the
O'Shea affair, which was then complicating all his
life. But (oddly enough) at his interview with him
at Brighton in November, 1890 — only a week before
the divorce trial — P. struck him as stronger in mind
and more statesmanlike than he had ever known him.

We agreed that he was infamously treated by his
own tail in Committee Room 15, and after; and that,
notwithstanding his incredible follies and vulgarities
since the split (which I put down to temporary loss
of equilibrium, both of mind and character) he had

[4] *See ante,* p. 138.

the strongest cards in his hand, and (as he said: "After another ten years! I am only forty-five"), he would probably have won. He was a man.

Harcourt has come back from his visit to Lancashire and Scotland very depressed. . . . Arnold Morley (the Chief Whip) agrees, and has impressed upon Harcourt that it will probably be a small majority, and without the Irish a minority.[5]

Home Rule must be kept in front. . . . As they were going together in a cab to W. H. Smith's funeral service last week, Harcourt said to J. M., slapping his knee: "My dear J. M., if I thought we were going to get a majority I would rather that both you and I were where old Smith is being put to-day." This, of course, only a passing mood: a creature of ups and downs.

[5] An accurate forecast.

CHAPTER XXXI

THE year 1891 witnessed a number of changes in the personnel of politics.

In March Lord Granville died; he had been for the lifetime of a generation the Liberal Leader in the House of Lords. He does not belong to the elusive figures in our political history, in the sense in which that term may be applied to Lord Shelburne and to Lord Melbourne. There were (one imagines) no folds or secret chambers in his temperament or character; but it is not very easy to get into relief his actual personality. He had the charm of manner of an accomplished man of the world; was a ready and even formidable debater, without perhaps reaching the first class; an indispensable member of every Liberal Cabinet; the most loyal and trusted of colleagues; and, with all his suaveness and seeming flexibility, a robust partisan, with convictions sincerely and tenaciously held. His father — known in the literature of biography as the fortunate correspondent of the most delightful of letter-writers, Lady Bessborough — was a diplomatist, who reached the highest posts in his profession, and was for a long time British Ambassador in Paris. It was in that atmosphere that the future

Liberal leader was bred. He succeeded to his title too young to have any experience worth the name in the House of Commons, but he was, for the best part of half a century, one of the most conspicuous figures in the House of Lords, always in a minority, but always holding his own; and once, when it seemed as if the two *enfants terribles* of the Liberal Party, Lord Palmerston and Lord John Russell, could not be brought to play in the same nursery, he was invited by Queen Victoria to form a Government.[1]

He was twice Foreign Secretary under Mr. Gladstone: from 1870 to 1874, when he had to deal with such delicate matters as the Alabama claims and British neutrality during the Franco-German War; and again, from 1880 to 1885, when the Egyptian problem, in its successive phases, taxed and overtaxed the wit of British statesmanship. Incidentally, he was one of the four Ministers (the others being Hartington, Northbrook and Dilke) who were primarily responsible (January, 1884) for Gordon's mission to the Sudan. In Mr. Gladstone's third Administration in February, 1886, he was content to see Lord Rosebery installed in his old office and to accept for himself that of Colonial Secretary.

It is difficult to conceive two men more radically different in origin, bringing-up, tastes, temperament, the angle of political and intellectual vision, than Gladstone and Granville. Yet when Granville died, after more than twenty years of the closest and most intimate association, Gladstone was bereaved, as he

[1] Morley, " Gladstone ", I, 625.

knew and felt, of the best friend he had in the world. Granville throughout had supplied the complementary qualities to his own, and though Gladstone was always the " predominant partner ", the other contributed invaluable assets in his cool, undazzled judgment and his unwavering personal devotion.

Parnell and W. H. Smith died on the same day — October 6, 1891 — and in the following December the death of the Duke of Devonshire removed Hartington from the House of Commons. The Duke was a man of considerable natural gifts, with a distinguished academic record, who, while zealously discharging during a long life the duties and responsibilities of a territorial magnate, preferred the *vita umbratilis* to the miry ways of politics.

The various leaderships, which were thus made vacant, were filled without any competition between rival claims. Lord Kimberley succeeded Lord Granville; Mr. John Redmond, on the threshold of a great parliamentary future, took command of the surviving handful of Parnellites; Mr. Chamberlain (some people called it the last stage in the " Rake's Progress ") stepped into the shoes of Lord Hartington; and Mr. Balfour, who was now universally recognized as gladiator in chief among the Tories *pur sang*, glided gracefully and inevitably into the seat of Mr. Smith.

CHAPTER XXXII

THE ELECTION OF 1892

IN the autumn of 1891, all parties were beginning to make active preparations for the general election. The setback in the electoral prospects of Home Rule in Great Britain, caused by the Parnellite split, was deemed to make it incumbent upon the managers of the Liberal Party to widen the area of their appeal. At the annual meeting of the National Liberal Federation, held in October at Newcastle, a syllabus of policy was produced, which became famous afterwards as the Newcastle Programme. It was a comprehensive and detailed catalogue of domestic reforms, from Welsh Disestablishment down to payment of members, which only a Liberal majority could be trusted to carry into law. It was, indeed, the forerunner of the elaborate party manifestos, which have since (unhappily, as I think) come to be regarded as the normal and necessary preliminaries to an election campaign. Mr. Gladstone himself was brought down to Newcastle to give it his general benediction. This he did in a somewhat perfunctory fashion; being in truth (he was now in his eighty-second year) indifferent to, not to say critical of, some of its items, and with the whole of his personal interest centred and absorbed in the completion of the last

task of his career — the establishment of Irish autonomy.[1]

Meanwhile, the Government were from time to
time engaged in getting on with such fragments of
their constructive Irish policy as survived the eclipse
of the author of the Dartford speech. In successive
sessions they extended the scope of Land Purchase,
by developments and amplifications of the Ashbourne
Acts. And in 1892 — the last year of the moribund
Parliament — they produced an Irish Local Government Bill, which never got beyond a second reading.
The stringent safeguards which it provided to meet
the dangers of tyrannical administration by the new
local authorities of the powers conferred on them
were known, in the political slang of the day, as the
" put-them-in-the-Dock " clauses.

A Small Holdings Bill was passed into law, in the
same year, to provide for the acquisition of land for
their creation by County Councils. The Liberal
Opposition sought in vain to substitute the Parish
for the County Council, and to give the Local Authority compulsory powers of purchase. Mr. Chamberlain declared against compulsion, on the ground that
it would wreck the chances of the measure.

A Woman's Suffrage Bill — introduced by private
members — was fortunate in the ballot, and came on
for second reading on April 27, 1892. To show the
diversity of the quarters from which the hostility to

[1] The accounts given of this Conference and Mr. Gladstone's part in
it, both by Lord Morley and Mr. Gardiner, in their Lives of Gladstone
and Harcourt, are exceptionally meagre. I cannot supplement them, as
under the disability of domestic sorrow I was not present.

this revolutionary change was at that time recruited, it may be interesting to preserve a copy of the "Whip" issued by the opponents of the Bill.

WOMEN'S SUFFRAGE BILL

The Second Reading of this Bill will be moved on APRIL 27.

You are earnestly requested to be present in the House of Commons, not later than 4.30, for the purpose of opposing the Motion.

H. H. Asquith	Geo. Hamilton
W. B. Barttelot	W. G. V. Harcourt
M. Hicks Beach	Henry James
J. L. Carew	H. Labouchere
J. Chamberlain	J. R. Mowbray
H. Chaplin	A. J. Mundella
R. Churchill	J. W. Pease
Geo. N. Curzon	J. A. Picton
T. G. Esmonde	Edward J. Reed
H. H. Fowler	M. W. Ridley

After a debate in which I remember I took part on one side, and Mr. George Wyndham on the other, the Bill was rejected by 175 to 152.

In June the end came, and Parliament was dissolved.

In the new House the composition of parties was as follows:

Liberal and Labour	274	Conservatives	269
Nationalists	81	Liberal Unionists	46
	355		315

The most notable new figure was that of Sir Charles Dilke, who had been absent from the previous Parliament. Dilke, the Canadian lawyer, and Michael Davitt, the ex-Fenian convict, entered the House for the first time.

Mr. Gladstone had shown portentous energy and powers of endurance during the campaign, and in a speech at Glasgow — otherwise pedestrian and almost tedious — had suddenly enraptured his audience, and enriched the records of English oratory, by his " Castor and Pollux " peroration.[2] He remained sanguine to the end, and for the figures of the polling in Midlothian, where his own majority was reduced from four thousand to six hundred and ninety, he seems to have been wholly unprepared. He did not, however, flinch for a moment, when the news came to him at luncheon at Dalmeny, and took Mr. Morley (who was a fellow guest) aside, to confide to him two new points — small and detailed — which had occurred to him about the Home Rule Bill. He had, indeed, other causes of depression which might well have daunted a man of smaller stature and less unquenchable courage. His deafness was growing steadily, and, as he told Mr. Morley during the same visit, he was apprehensive of cataract in one eye and of specks in the other. " The doors of the senses," he said, in words which have a terribly pathetic ring, " are gradually closing." [3] But

[2] Set out in an Appendix in " Gladstone ", III, 562.

[3] What precedes is taken from a conversation which I had with Mr. Morley, recorded in my diary, July 23, 1892.

he was as convinced as ever that it was not for him (in Cicero's fine phrase) *" injussu Imperatoris, id est Dei, a statione discedere."* [4]

So he determined to fight on — until that missive of discharge should come.

[4] " Without an order from his Commander, God Himself, to quit his post."

PART TWO

CHAPTER XXXIII

THE LAST GLADSTONE GOVERNMENT, 1892–1894

IN view of the small dimensions and the composite character of the adverse majority, the Salisbury Government, instead of following the precedents of 1868, 1874, and 1880, and resigning at once, resolved to meet the new House of Commons.

I was engaged (August 2) in conducting a case at the Old Bailey — a rare experience with me — when I received a letter from Mr. Gladstone inviting me to move, on the part of the Liberal Opposition, an amendment to the Address. It was to be a direct vote of want of confidence, and to consist (in Mr. Gladstone's words) " as far as possible, in a single operation avoiding extraneous matter."

The Amendment which I actually moved on August 8 was upon these lines. It was seconded by Mr. Burt, and after three days' debate it was carried (August 11) by a majority of forty, the numbers being 350 against 310.

The Government thereupon resigned and Mr. Gladstone accepted the task of forming for the fourth time a new Administration.

The business of Cabinet construction, with its attendant " butcheries ", was at once set on foot, Mr.

Gladstone being assisted in the mechanical part of the task by his two old private secretaries — Sir Algernon West and Spencer Lyttelton.

On Sunday afternoon, August 14, I was at Brooks' Club, when Spencer Lyttelton came in, and gave me the letter from Mr. Gladstone, of which a facsimile will be found on the following pages.

I replied at once, gratefully accepting the Prime Minister's proposal, which opened the door of the Cabinet to me just before my fortieth birthday. I may therefore not inappropriately say at this stage a word about my personal position.

I had found, during the preceding year, from conversations with Mr. Morley and others who were in Mr. Gladstone's confidence, that it was fairly certain that, if the Liberals were in the majority and were able to form a Government, I should be offered a place in it. I had shortly before (February, 1890) taken what is always a hazardous step in a barrister's life — applied for and been granted " Silk." The risk turned out to have been justified by the event. It was, in the circumstances, not unlikely that I might have the refusal of one of the law officerships. The prospect did not attract me, as I had no judicial ambitions; though much interested in law, I was more interested in politics; and the advice of one or two friends, on whose judgment I felt I could rely — Mr. Balfour was one of them — confirmed my own opinion that if I joined the new Government it should be in some political office. Sir W. Harcourt, with whom I discussed the matter, professed to prefer law

Secret

Hawarden Castle,
Chester.

W.E.G.

Aug 14. 92

My dear Asquith

I have the pleasure
of writing to propose that you
should allow me to submit
your name to Her Majesty
for the office of Home Secretary.

I have understood that
you are willing to quit
your practice at the bar

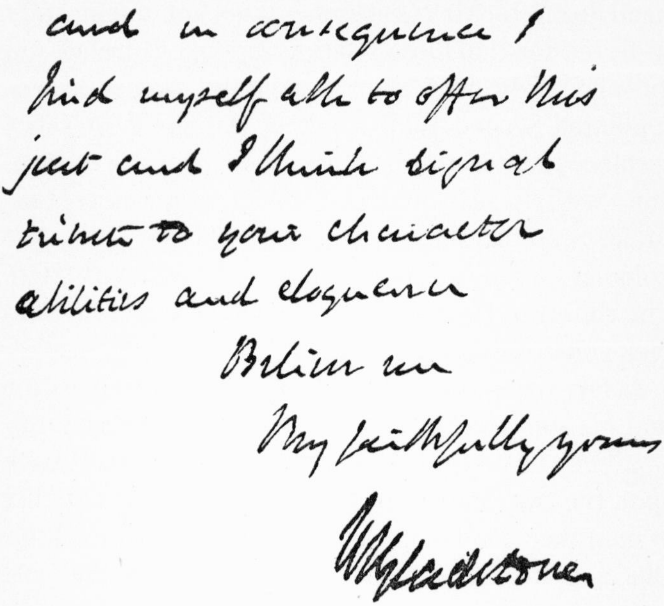

[handwritten letter]

and in consequence I find myself able to offer this just and I think signal tribute to your character abilities and eloquence

Believe me

My faithfully yours

W. Gladstone

to politics, and to regret having left his old profession, *sed quaere*.

I had become equally determined not to join a Government in which there was not a strong infusion of new blood. I was satisfied from my conversations with Mr. Morley that this was now assured. The little group already described, who were on the best of terms with Morley, and also, though in a less intimate sense, with Harcourt, who was wont to chasten those whom he loved, had hoped that a new departure would be marked by the appointment of Acland as Chief Whip. This suggestion, however, did not commend itself to Mr. Gladstone, who not unnaturally preferred for that close relationship an old friend and colleague, Edward Marjoribanks. But Tom Ellis was appointed Second Whip. Acland was given an office peculiarly suited to him, that of Minister of Education, with a seat in the Cabinet. Two important Under-Secretaryships — Foreign Affairs and the Colonies — fell to Edward Grey and Sydney Buxton. The claims of the " young men " were thus fully and even generously acknowledged.

A few days later Mr. Gladstone proposed to me that his son, Herbert, should be my Under-Secretary — a very flattering mark of confidence. I look back upon the two years, during which we served together in unbroken confidence and coöperation at the Home Office, as the pleasantest, and in some ways the most satisfactory, in a long administrative life.

The process of Cabinet-making was conducted in Lord Rendel's house in Carlton Gardens, where Mr. Gladstone sat in an inner sanctum with Harcourt and Morley as assessors. The great difficulty was about Lord Rosebery, whose decision was in doubt till the end; indeed, it was not till Mr. Gladstone was in the train on his way to Osborne, that a monosyllabic telegram arrived from Dalmeny — " So be it, R." Sir W. Harcourt went to see Rosebery the next day; " found him very cheerful," and they had a " long talk as if nothing had happened ", is the entry in

Lewis Harcourt's " Journal." [1] It was in the course of this conversation that Harcourt made to Rosebery the characteristic remark: " Without you, the Government would have been ridiculous; with you, it is only possible." [2]

Harcourt grumbled that so many of the important offices were to be given to peers, and when Mr. Gladstone justified this on the ground of the importance of strengthening the numerically weak Liberal minority in that House, he replied that " you might as well try to strengthen the Ocean by pouring into it a *petit verre* of cognac." [3]

Mr. Gladstone, who was fond of familiar faces, insisted, against the remonstrances of both Harcourt and Morley, on making Lord Ripon Colonial Secretary. The two fighting departments were put in the capable hands of Lord Spencer and Campbell-Bannerman. Who could have foreseen that they were destined to be the innocent causes, the one of Mr. Gladstone's resignation, the other of the fall of the Government?

Fowler, who thought, and perhaps justly, that he deserved a more exalted place in the hierarchy, was given the Local Government Board, where (as was shown by his admirable conduct of the Parish Councils Bill) his special talents and experience found a congenial field.

There was the usual and inevitable trouble about

[1] Gardiner, II, 182.
[2] This is the form in which he repeated it to me; it is given in slightly different words in Lewis Harcourt's " Journal ".
[3] *Ibid.*, p. 183.

Photograph by Russell of London

THE MARQUIS OF RIPON

the " last man in." One of the candidates for the
post, who was getting anxious about his chances,
came to John Morley (who told me the tale) for encouragement, and was unlucky enough to find him in
rather a ragged mood.

J.M.: " My dear X., *if* you get into the Cabinet,
take my advice and never open your lips there."

X.: " I never do, except when I have something to
say."

J.M.: " That's just when you should keep them
shut."

When completed, the Cabinet consisted of seventeen members, the newcomers (besides Acland and
myself) being Fowler, Bryce, and Arnold Morley.

The new Government kissed hands and received
their seals at Osborne on August 18, and during the
next six months were engaged in becoming familiar
with their offices and with one another and in preparing for their first parliamentary session.

CHAPTER XXXIV

THE SECOND HOME RULE BILL, 1893

LORD MORLEY records in his " Recollections ", some time in the first of the troubled years of this Government and its immediate successor, that, in the course of conversation, he and I agreed that a worse stroke of luck than such a majority has never befallen political leaders.[1]

The continuance for three years of the two Liberal Governments which held office from 1892 to 1895 is indeed one of the miracles of parliamentary history. The ostensible majority of forty was made up entirely by counting in the Irish Nationalists, who were themselves split up into two mutually hostile forces — Parnellites and anti-Parnellites. The Parnellites, though numerically a mere handful, were led by an exceptionally able parliamentarian, and while equally faithful with their colleagues to the cause of Home Rule, they felt bound to reëcho from time to time their dead leader's professed suspicions of English good faith, and to embarrass the path of the old comrades who had deserted Parnell in the hour of need. One illustration out of many that might be given will suffice.

[1] " Recollections ", I, 374.

In the course of the interminable discussion in the committee stage of the Home Rule Bill of 1893, on the position of the Irish Members, after Home Rule, in the Imperial Parliament, when the respective merits or demerits of total exclusion, " in and out " retention, or retention *omnes omnia* (in the jargon of the day), were exhaustively canvassed, the Government had declared in favour of retention in the reduced number of eighty. Mr. John Redmond proposed to substitute for eighty the full Irish representation of one hundred and three. The Unionists were known to to ready to support him in the hope of killing the Bill. The anti-Parnellites were naturally in sore straits, and it was with wry faces and perhaps unquiet consciences that a sufficient number of them were rallied into the division lobby to save the Government from defeat. As it was, the Government majority did not exceed fourteen.

It was to this kind of hazard that we were constantly exposed, and on some of our measures, such as the Welsh Disestablishment Bill, the majority would now and again sink to seven.

The mandate for which the party had appealed to the electorate was to get through with Home Rule, and so much as could be achieved of the Newcastle Programme. This meant legislation on a large scale and over a wide field. How was such legislation possible, with a composite and precarious majority in the House of Commons, and against an implacable and overwhelming Opposition in the House of Lords?

The first and most imperative call was that of

Home Rule. Early in the autumn of 1892 a small Cabinet Committee was appointed — Mr. Gladstone, Herschell, Spencer, J. Morley, Bryce and Campbell-Bannerman — and for months it grappled with the details of the forthcoming Bill, which was at last introduced (February 13, 1893) by Mr. Gladstone in the House of Commons.

Its discussion occupied the House for eighty sittings, spread over six months, notwithstanding in the later stages a free use of the closure and the guillotine. It was not read a third time till September first. It may be interesting by way of comparison to record that the Act of Union, which destroyed the Irish Parliament, took thirteen days; the Reform Bill of 1831, forty-seven days; the Repeal of the Corn Laws, ten; and the Disestablishment of the Irish Church, nineteen.

Mr. Gladstone's speech in introducing the Bill lasted for two and a quarter hours, and was a prodigious physical and intellectual performance for a man of his years. But though it contained fine passages in his most characteristic vein, it was not on the same level as an oratorical masterpiece with some of his previous efforts. There were indeed, so far as my recollection goes, no really great speeches in the full-dress debates on the Bill. This was partly due to the fact that, after nearly eight years of active controversy, there was, in the region of principle, nothing new to be said. But apart from that the truth is that an air of unreality brooded over the discussion. Every one knew — if I may quote an expression of

my own, which became a catchword of the platform
— that we were " ploughing the sands." Whatever
was done with the Bill in the House of Commons, it
was certain that when it got to the House of Lords it
would receive the shortest of shrifts, and all our
labours would be thrown away.

It became a Committee struggle, and during that
stage, which lasted forty-seven days, points large and
small were raised and amendments serious and frivo-
lous were moved, just as though the House were
dealing with the structure of a potential Act of Parliament.

It was really Mr. Chamberlain's session, and in the
whole of his career that great debater never displayed
with more versatility and effect his extraordinary
powers of parliamentary swordplay. It must be admitted that such a question as that already referred
to — the retention of the Irish Members — upon
which the Government were driven from one solution
to another, gave priceless material to a master of
dialectic.

Mr. Chamberlain's root objection to the first Home
Rule Bill had been that it excluded the Irish Members from the Imperial Parliament. This he had
described as the " Key of the position." The second
Home Rule Bill sought to get rid of the objection by
proposing to retain them. But that only enabled Mr.
Chamberlain to unmask a new set of batteries. Were
the Members to be retained in full, or only in reduced
numbers? For all purposes, including English and
Scotch business? Or only for Imperial business? How

were you to draw the line? And what was to be the position of a Government which might be in a majority one night and in a minority the next?

The " in and out method ", which was the original proposal made tentatively in the Bill, was not only riddled with criticism by Chamberlain and others, but found little favour in any quarter. The Government then suggested that the Irish Members should be retained with unlimited voting power. " What will that come to? " asked Chamberlain. " That the interests of Great Britain are to be controlled by delegates nominated by priests, elected by illiterates subsidized by the enemies of their country? "

The Solicitor-General, Sir John Rigby, one of the leaders of the Chancery Bar, whose burly figure and bluff, bucolic manner had made him a favourite with the House, was helpless in single combat with such an antagonist. But even the " dreary drip " of prolonged and sterile debate did not extinguish the passions which now and again broke through the surface.

When, after forty-seven days of Committee the " guillotine " was applied at ten o'clock in the evening of July 27, there arose (largely through the maladroit handling of the situation by the Chairman) a tumult which soon developed in some quarters into a free fight. Lord R. Churchill, I myself, and some others, tried in vain to induce Members on both sides to go into the Division Lobbies. At last the Speaker (Peel) was sent for. After two or three minutes he entered and took the Chair, throwing his robe about him with his most majestic air, and for a moment glared around, without saying a word, upon the House, now silent and abashed. Mr. Gladstone looked on with an expression of pained and incredulous bewilderment, and Members dispersed, many of them with hangdog and discomfited looks, to their homes.[2]

At last, in September, the Bill got to the House of Lords and succumbed at once to the sentence of doom which had all along awaited it. The debate was short in duration, and not very striking in the quality of the speeches. But the peers, who had trooped to Westminster, known and unknown, from all points of the compass, had come not to listen but to vote. Out of 560 on the roll, 419 voted against the Bill and 41 for it.

And the 419 went back to the places whence they had come with the proud conviction that they had saved their country, and killed Home Rule.

[2] The scene was painful and humiliating enough to those who loved the House of Commons, but as it made excellent " copy " its ugly features were exaggerated and over-painted by " descriptive " writers at the time. I happened to have a small dinner party at the House earlier in the evening, and I took one of my guests, a distinguished foreigner who had never been inside the House, into the Gallery. I met him a day or two afterwards, and I began to apologize, when he exclaimed in surprise: " Why, I have been in almost every legislative chamber in Europe, and I have always seen the same thing! "

CHAPTER XXXV

MR. GLADSTONE'S LAST SESSION, 1893–1894

IN the sphere of administration, Ministers had a freer hand. My own department, the Home Office, was an extraordinary conglomerate of diverse and disconnected functions. The Secretary of State combined the duties of Minister of Justice (there was then no Court of Criminal Appeal); Minister of Labour (mines, factories, workshops, etc.; railways were under the Board of Trade); Minister of Police for the Metropolis, with vague and ill-defined jurisdiction over the provincial police authorities, arising partly from custom, and partly from his power to withold the Government grant; and Minister of Prisons, Reformatories, and Industrial Schools. Incidentally, he was supposed to keep an eye on the Channel Islands and the Isle of Man.

There was enough here to satisfy the most voracious appetite for work. In important matters, such, for example, as the increased efficiency of Factory Inspection [1] and the initiation of more humane and rational prison methods, it was found possible, in advance of fresh legislation, to make substantial progress by administrative action.

[1] See Note at end of chapter.

The Education Office and the Board of Trade were among the departments which offered the greatest administrative opportunities, and full advantage was taken of them by Mr. Acland and Mr. Mundella. Notwithstanding the Free Education Act, nearly one fifth of the elementary schools in England and Wales were still charging fees. Acland insisted that the education given should be really free. Campbell-Bannerman introduced the eight-hour day, without reduction of wages, in the ordnance factory at Woolwich, with such successful results that the example was followed by other departments, and the State began by modest but effective steps to assume the character of a " model employer."

The last session of Mr. Gladstone's active parliamentary life was, and still remains, the longest on record. It extended from January, 1893, to March, 1894. For, apart from Home Rule, attempts were made by the Government — in pursuance of the pledges given in the Newcastle Programme — to deal with two urgent domestic problems: Employers' Liability, and the development of a more democratic system of local government in England and Wales by the establishment of Parish Councils. In both cases the House of Commons was brought into sharp collision with the House of Lords. The Employers' Liability Bill (for which I was responsible) sought to get rid of the doctrine of " common employment ", and to put an injured workman on the same footing as regards legal redress, whether the negligence which caused the injury was that of a fellow workman or of a third person. It foundered, after many attempts at accommodation, on the rock of " contracting out."

The Parish Councils Bill, which was in the capable and conciliatory hands of Mr. Fowler, occupied nearly fifty days in the House of Commons. It was not directly opposed in the House of Lords, but their amendments were of such a restrictive and belittling character that it was not without many doubts that the Government, in the end, assented to them to save the Bill.

Mr. Gladstone not only shared those doubts, but although he had then (January, 1894) provisionally resigned, he urged upon his colleagues from his retirement at Biarritz that there should be an immediate dissolution, whereby, still under his leadership, they could appeal to the country to decide the issue, which of the two Houses was to prevail. The suggestion found no support in the Cabinet; whether as a matter of tactics he or they were right is, and must always remain, a highly debatable question. He bowed to the inevitable; his determination to resign became a fixed resolve; and, on March 1, 1894, still speaking as the head and mouthpiece of the Government, he made his last speech in the House of Commons. After announcing their reluctant acceptance of the changes made by the Lords in the Parish Councils Bill, he went on:

" We are compelled to accompany that acceptance with the sorrowful declaration that the differences, not of a temporary or casual nature merely, but differences of conviction, differences of prepossession,

differences of mental habit, and differences of fundamental tendency, between the House of Lords and
the House of Commons, appear to have reached a
development in the present year such as to create a
state of things of which we are compelled to say that,
in our judgment, it cannot continue. Sir, I do not
wish to use hard words, which are easily employed
and as easily retorted — it is a game that two can
play at — but without using hard words, without
presuming to judge of motives, without desiring or
venturing to allege imputations, I have felt it a duty
to state what appeared to me to be indisputable facts.
The issue which is raised between a deliberative
assembly, elected by the votes of more than six million people, and a deliberative assembly occupied by
many men of virtue, by many men of talent, of course
with considerable diversities and varieties, is a controversy which, when once raised, must go forward
to an issue. The issue has been postponed, long postponed, I rejoice to say; it has been postponed, in
many cases to a considerable degree, by that discretion, circumspection, and reserve in the use of enormous privileges which the House of Lords, on various
occasions in my recollection, in the time of the Duke
of Wellington, Lord Aberdeen, and other periods,
have shown. But I am afraid that the epoch, the age
of that reserve and circumspection, may have gone
by. I will not abandon all hope of it, but although
I do not like to say that the situation now is intolerable — because that is a hard, and may seem a dicta-
torial word — I think honourable gentlemen opposite

must feel, as I feel, that in some way or other a
solution will have to be found for this tremendous
contrariety and incessant conflict, upon matters of
high principle and profound importance, between the
representatives of the people and those who fill a
nominated or non-elected Chamber."

This was his valedictory message to the House of
Commons, and the legacy which he left to his party.

NOTE

(*Factory Inspection*)

To show how backward things were, I may quote
from a minute which I circulated to the Cabinet in
December, 1893.

Referring to my memorandum of December, 1892,
the changes then proposed and subsequently sanctioned have now been in operation for several months.
They were of a tentative and experimental character,
and have been fully justified by the results. But we
are still inadequately equipped for the effective exe-
cution of the law, and I deem it an urgent duty to
press without delay for the means of further improving the system of Inspection. Both the staff (eighty-
six) and the expenditure are still upon an extremely
modest scale.

Two ladies were appointed, one for London and
the other for Glasgow. I cannot express too highly
my sense of the beneficial results which have followed
this experiment. The law has been enforced in industries where women are exclusively or mainly employed, with a vigilance and a stringency which was
previously impossible, and with the best conse-

quences. But there are large areas of the country which the two lady inspectors cannot possibly find time to visit. I propose to appoint two additional Female Inspectors.

The new class of officers, Inspectors' Assistants, created also for the first time last year, has done excellent service, but it is still inadequate in number for the work. I propose to add ten to the existing number of fifteen.

It was with some trepidation that I sent in this modest demand to the Chancellor of the Exchequer. As Mr. Gardiner says,[2] " the formidable bark of the watchdog at the Treasury penetrated all the offices in Whitehall alike." But, perhaps because Harcourt had a lingering weakness for his own old office, he accepted my proposals without even a momentary snarl.

[2] " Harcourt ", III, 202.

CHAPTER XXXVI

FORMATION OF THE ROSEBERY GOVERNMENT, 1894

GLADSTONE was made to resign by his colleagues, and Morley was the mouthpiece of this ultimatum." With all the respect that is due to the writer, I must characterize this as an erroneous version of a great historical event.

Mr. Gladstone's resignation was entirely his own act; its immediate occasion was a difference of opinion between himself and the colleague whom he valued most, Lord Spencer, on the Navy Estimates; and his intention was contingently declared to the Cabinet early in January, 1894 (on the ninth), if those estimates were to be persisted in and supported by them. Between that date and February 28, when his retirement was finally announced to them, though some of his colleagues (of whom I was one) were of opinion that, if his determination was fixed, it was in the general interest that its publication should not be delayed, we all of us, severally and collectively, did everything in our power (short of yielding on the Estimates) [1] to induce him to remain. As to Mr. Morley's so-called " ultimatum ", it consisted in his

---

[1] I have purposely not gone into the question of the merits or demerits of the Navy Estimates. All the materials for a judgment are to be found in Gardiner's " Harcourt ", II, ch. xiv.

undertaking, at Mr. Gladstone's own request, the delicate task of breaking the news to Mrs. Gladstone.

It is quite true that, during the six weeks which elapsed between the two dates mentioned above, Mr. Gladstone, who spent most of the time at Biarritz, was still not without hopes of bringing round his colleagues to his own view on the Navy issue. A letter from Sir E. Hamilton to Harcourt [2] (January 29) gives a vivid picture of his state of mind at the time.

I have seen Acton to-day, who has just arrived from Biarritz. He fully confirms what West said, as to Mr. Gladstone's great excitability and the fierceness of his mood, and I understand that he won't admit the possibility of any change of mind. But there are considerations which make one think that the door is still ajar. He is apparently catching at straws, doubts the absolute unanimity of his colleagues against him, and so forth. . . .

It was while he was a prey to these perturbing thoughts, that he believed he saw a way of escape (as has been described in the last chapter) in an immediate dissolution. It was only when he found his colleagues as unamenable on this point as on the other, that his resolution crystallized. It was in this sense, no doubt, that, when at the last moment Harcourt was protesting against his retirement, he exclaimed "Not retirement! I have been put out." [3] He was disappointed, and indeed for the moment incensed; and he used afterwards — half jocularly, half angrily

2 "Harcourt", II, 254.   3 *Ibid.*, p. 262.

— to speak of his final leave-taking with his colleagues, on March 1, as the " blubbering Cabinet." Before the Cabinet separated, Lord Kimberley (the senior member), who was genuinely moved, had uttered a few broken sentences of affection and reverence, when Harcourt produced from his box and proceeded to read a well-thumbed MS. of highly elaborated eulogy. Of those who were present there are now few survivors; but which of them can forget the expression of Mr. Gladstone's face, as he looked on with hooded eyes and tightened lips at this maladroit performance?

He had just entered on his eighty-fifth year; the " doors of the senses ", in his own tragic phrase, were " closing " fast; and even though, as his last speech (on the same March 1) in the House of Commons proves, there was as yet no extinction of the " wonted fires ", yet he must have been tempted at times to utter the prayer:

> " Let me not live. . . .
> After my flame lacks oil, to be the snuff
> Of younger spirits." [4]

The retirement of the greatest figure in politics was the signal for letting loose of the waters. It is well known that (notwithstanding the controversy about the Navy) it was Mr. Gladstone's intention to recommend Lord Spencer as his successor. By a strange omission, at his final audience, Queen Victoria

[4] " All's Well That Ends Well ", Act I, Sc. ii.

did not ask his advice, or even broach the subject. On March 3 she asked Lord Rosebery to form a Government, and he accepted her invitation. He was already in effect assured that he could count upon the coöperation of all the members of Mr. Gladstone's late Cabinet, with the possible exception of Sir W. Harcourt. To him he at once offered the leadership of the House of Commons, at the same time informing him that he regarded Lord Kimberley as his own fittest successor at the Foreign Office, and that he did not see any person in the House of Commons who was so suitable for the post.

The following day, at a further interview, " I told him," said Harcourt, " that, apart from his condition as a peer, I admitted Lord Kimberley to be the fittest person (for Foreign Secretary), and that I could not designate any special person in the House of Commons to occupy the post. The point, therefore, to be considered was how, assuming Lord Kimberley to go to the Foreign Office, the Leader of the House of Commons might be secured in that privity to all that was taking place in foreign affairs, in which it was essential that he should have a voice. I said that I was of opinion that the Foreign Secretary should communicate as fully and freely with the Leader of the House of Commons as he did with the Prime Minister. To this Lord Rosebery agreed." [5]

[5] Gardiner, " Harcourt ", II, 272. I may say that I thought at the time, as I do now, that Harcourt's was a perfectly reasonable request. The conditions — a peer Prime Minister and a peer Foreign Secretary — have only once occurred since; in Lord Salisbury's third Government, 1895–1902, when Mr. Balfour was Leader of the House of Commons. In

Thereupon Sir W. Harcourt agreed to serve under Lord Rosebery as Leader of the House of Commons.[6]

The causes and consequences of Harcourt's super-session by Rosebery at this juncture will always remain a piquant, and perhaps a baffling, subject of speculation to those who are interested in the personal aspects of political history.

There is no question that the man whose direct personal influence had most to do with the result was Harcourt's most intimate and confidential political associate — John Morley, from whom the younger Harcourt had, only two years before, received an assurance that, in this very event, he would support his father as against Lord Rosebery for the leadership.

Harcourt and Morley were in all ways an incongruous couple. They belonged not only to different generations, but in all essentials, except that of actual chronology, to different centuries. Both of them were men of high and rare cultivation; on the intellectual side, Morley was what Harcourt most loathed, an *idéologue,* and Harcourt was what jarred most upon Morley, a Philistine. Harcourt, with a supposed in-

---

the Liberal Government which came into office in 1905, and over which Sir H. Campbell-Bannerman and I successively presided, both Prime Minister and Foreign Secretary were in the House of Commons.

[6] Morley was much put out when he heard of the arrangement actually come to. He appears to have understood that Harcourt would stipulate that the Foreign Secretary should be in the House of Commons, and he did not at all agree that there was no person in that House as " suitable " for the post as Kimberley. He was offered the India Office; or the presidency of the Council, but declined both; and retired, not in the best of moods, into what he called his " back kitchen " — the Irish Office.

fusion (however diluted) of Plantagenet blood; the grandson of a Georgian Archbishop; brought up with the tastes and habits of the caste in which he was born; but a natural mutineer, with a really powerful intelligence, a mordant wit, and a masculine and challenging personality, soon shook off his hereditary fetters, and seemed at one time to be in training for the post of the great Condottiere of the political world.[7] Morley, sprung from the Lancashire middle class, dipped but not dyed in the waters of Oxford, a youthful acolyte of Mill, had hovered for a time around the threshold of the Comtean conventicle; but was best known, when he turned his face from pure literature to political journalism, as the expositor of Voltaire and Rousseau and the Encyclopædists of France. Political exigencies make strange stable companions, but rarely two, to all appearance, less well assorted than these. They had hardly even a prejudice in common. Their intercourse, once they became friends, was chequered by periodic misunderstandings. Both, in their several ways, were creatures of moods and tenses; but their correspondence — for both were excellent letter-writers — is full of interest and charm. Had they a common political faith? It is hard to say — except that, from different points of view, they were equally ardent disciples of what used then to be called the Anti-Imperialist and " Little England " school. It was almost by pure accident that, at the beginning of 1886, they found

[7] The leader whom he would have found most congenial to his taste was undoubtedly Disraeli.

themselves side by side in the Home Rule Camp, and within a few months became the two recognized lieutenants of Mr. Gladstone. They were neither of them orthodox Gladstonians of long standing. It was not many years since Morley had described the Great Man's mind as a " busy mint of logical counterfeits ",[8] and Harcourt had declared, when Jingoism was lying on its death-bed, that " there must be no return from Elba." It is open to doubt whether Harcourt was ever at any stage a convinced believer in Home Rule (except as a desperate alternative to coercion), and he never had any faith in Parnell. It was quite otherwise with Morley. In the middle of the dirt-slinging and general disillusionment which followed the eclipse of Parnell, Morley writes to Harcourt: [9] " The crash to me is worse than to you. I *believed in this policy*,[10] and I have had some opinion of Parnell, though no illusions."

Notwithstanding these incompatibilities, the two men coöperated loyally between 1890 and 1892 to strengthen Mr. Gladstone's hands, and to get the Newcastle Programme on to its legs. After the election of 1892, they sat together on his right hand and his left in the inner sanctum at Carlton Gardens, at the apportionment of the loaves and fishes in the new Government. Their personal relations continued for a time to be fairly smooth, until they came to a violent quarrel over the financial clauses of the Home

8 " Struggle for National Education ", Morley, 1873.
9 January 7, 1891, " Harcourt ", II, 95.
10 The italics are mine.

Rule Bill of 1893. Harcourt had written a strongly worded remonstrance to Mr. Gladstone on the morning of the introduction of the Bill (February 12, 1893); upon which Morley comments: " That you should have, on such a morning, written as you have done to Mr. G. is the kind of thing that Brougham would have done, and nobody else that I have read of in modern public life." [11]

The comparison, in this angry outburst, of Harcourt to Brougham is unhappily only too apposite. Both were men of the highest gifts, head and shoulders above almost all their contemporaries; but in both cases the gifts of nature were rendered dangerous, and even ruinous to their possessors from inherent defects of temperament, which neither of them had the power, or perhaps the will, to overcome.

There was something essentially lovable about Harcourt's nature; the nature of a great breezy, elemental, ungovernable child who had never grown up. He was the best of husbands and fathers, and he had a vein of tenderness, which showed itself in the quickest and warmest sympathy when any of his friends were hit hard in the vicissitudes of life by bereavement or domestic anxieties. He could be a delightful, if somewhat overpowering, companion; was a keen, but not malevolent, observer of other men's foibles; wholly without personal jealousy; and generously and even lavishly appreciative of any piece of good work, whether done by a colleague or a member of the rank and file. And yet, to tell the naked truth,

[11] " Harcourt ", II, 221.

he was an almost impossible colleague, and would
have been a wholly impossible Chief. This, I believe, would have been the overwhelming verdict of
the members of Mr. Gladstone's last Cabinet.[12]

Mr. Morley, in the course which he took, was really
acting as the exponent of the general will of those
immediately concerned. He had his own special
reasons for soreness, but he knew his colleagues well
enough to be fully aware that (even if he had desired
it) a Harcourt Government was out of the range of
practical politics. Nor was it a question of a Cabal
in the inner circle. " When the crisis came he (Harcourt) was almost entirely deserted by the Liberal
newspapers, which either dismissed his claims openly,
or, as in the case of the *Daily News* and the *Westminster Gazette,* appealed to him to perform hara-
kiri and win for himself a deathless name." [13] There
was grumbling in the Radical group in the House of
Commons, who disliked a " Peer-Premier ", and some
bewilderment in the ranks of the party in the country, that the Great Gladiator, now in his sixty-seventh
year, should be passed over in favour of a man twenty
years his junior, with no corresponding record of
parliamentary service. But, on the whole, the accession of Lord Rosebery to the chief place was received, if not with enthusiasm, at least with acquiescence and hope.

[12] The statement alleged to have been made by Morley to Lewis
Harcourt that " all the Cabinet in the House of Commons with the
possible exception of Asquith and Acland (not alluding to himself —
J. M.) were in favour of W. V. H. as Prime Minister " is quite fan-
tastically wide of the mark. (" Harcourt ", II, 269.)

[13] *Ibid.*, p. 267.

CHAPTER XXXVII

THE Rosebery Administration was afflicted from the first by an internal malady which from time to time threatened to prove fatal in its efficiency and even to its existence. Lord Rosebery in his monograph on Pitt, describing the relations between Fox and Shelburne [1] in 1873, had written as follows:

It would be too much to maintain that all the members of a Cabinet should feel an implicit confidence in each other.

But between a Prime Minister in the House of Lords and the leader of the House of Commons such a confidence is indispensable. Responsibility rests so largely with the one, and articulation so greatly with the other, that unity of sentiment is the one necessary link that makes a relation, in any case difficult, in any way possible. The voice of Jacob and the hands of Esau may effect a successful imposture but can hardly constitute a durable Administration.[2]

This " necessary link " between the two leaders in 1894-1895 never came into being. The arrangement already described in regard to the Foreign Office

---

[1] In " Sybil " Mr. Disraeli describes Lord Shelburne as " one of the suppressed characters of English history."

[2] Quoted by Sir A. West, who sent the passage to Mr. Gladstone.

might have been made to work, if there had been
" unity of sentiment " between the principal persons
concerned. The questions of foreign policy which
from time to time arose — Siam, Nicaragua, etc. —
were not (with the exception of the control of the
headwaters of the Nile) of first-rate importance, but
there were few of them in the handling of which by
the Foreign Office the keen scent of Harcourt failed
to detect the symptoms of the abomination which he
detested of all others — a " Forward Policy." The
unflagging industry and the unfailing copiousness
with which from day to day he assailed Lord Kimberley made that unhappy man's life an almost intolerable burden. I can speak with the more freedom
because on the merits of most of the points at issue I
was disposed to side with Harcourt; but his lack of
any sense of proportion, his incapacity for self-re-
straint, and his perverse delight in inflaming and
embittering every controversy, made coöperation
with him always difficult and often impossible. Cabinet life under such conditions was a weariness both
to the flesh and the spirit. I must add my testimony
to that of Campbell-Bannerman, whose flashes of
cynical humour now and again lightened the scene,
that the Prime Minister himself rarely failed in
patience and good nature. Campbell-Bannerman
writes to his brother (February 12, 1895):

Two things against us:
1. The Irish hard up to maintain their poor fellows
hanging on here.
2. Intrigues of Dilke and Labby, and sulks and

despondency of a certain great man of my near acquaintance.

The last is very bad and is the cause of woes innumerable. The Prime Minister is most patient and good-natured, but his difficulties on this ground are prodigious. *There are no other difficulties.*[3]

During the greater part of 1894 the two leaders were barely on speaking terms.

A notable and melancholy illustration of the pass which things had reached came very soon. Mr. Gladstone's farewell speech in the House of Commons had been a direct appeal to his old party to concentrate their forces upon a campaign against the veto of the House of Lords. Sir W. Harcourt himself, a few weeks before at Derby, had raised the same cry.[4] We had been (he said) too long a peer-ridden nation; the time was at hand when the " issue as to whether the Commons or the Lords should prevail " must be tried. He quoted with gusto Mr. Chamberlain's question in a speech at Denbigh ten years before: " Are you going to be governed by yourselves, or will you submit to an oligarchy which is the mere accident of birth? " And his declaration: " The chronicles of the House of Lords are one long record of concessions delayed until they have lost their grace, of rights denied until extorted from their fears."

Lord Rosebery, as in duty bound, was ready to take up the mission bequeathed to him by his predecessor. But he soon found that he would have to

[3] Spender's " Life of Campbell-Bannerman ", I, 166.
[4] " Harcourt ", II, 255.

reckon without the active support of his two principal colleagues who were gradually patching up their
own quarrel. "I entirely concur with you," writes
Harcourt to Morley in September, 1894, "in the
opinion that under the present circumstances, and
with the Government as at present constituted, it is
simply ridiculous to talk of tackling the House of
Lords." [5] He himself was determined to raise the
banner of Local Option, while "Mr. Morley's main
interest at the time was the assertion of the claims of
Home Rule as the main commitment of the party." [6]
So both these eminent men held deliberately aloof
from the campaign.

Lord Spencer who, with his high sense of the traditions and obligations of colleagueship, appears to
have remonstrated, received from Harcourt (September 21) a remarkable reply: " I don't know why you
should suppose I shall depart from my fixed resolution not to make any public speech. Why should I?
You and your friends have informed me sufficiently
frankly you do not regard me as fit to lead. Why,
then, should I pretend to take the initiative only in
order that you may repudiate me? As you know, I
am not a supporter of the present Government. I
have a great personal regard for all of you, and contemplate your proceedings with an impartial curiosity and a benevolent neutrality. I quite agree that
your position is a difficult one, and I wish you well
out of it. But I see that your leader is announced
for a good many speeches in which he will, no

[5] "Harcourt", II, 307.   [6] *Ibid.*, p. 344.

doubt, develop his policy with his accustomed clearness — and then you will know what to think and do." [7]

Lord Spencer's rejoinder was simple — and crushing:

" What you say on politics is sad, and I hope your mood will change. You embarked on the ship, and you are too important to be anything but an active leader of the crew. How can you stand by when important operations have to be considered? "

In the meantime (such is the irony of things), in this same year, 1894, the Rosebery Administration had, through the agency of Harcourt himself, established an enduring claim to fame by a legislative achievement of the highest class. The Budget of 1894, which embodied new and far-reaching principles of taxation, bitterly derided at the time, but never since departed from by any Chancellor of the Exchequer of any party, was Harcourt's handiwork. [8] He piloted it, almost unaided, through the shoals and reefs of Committee and Report in the House of Commons with unfailing adroitness and imperturbable temper. During the whole course of its progress it was his boast (though there was not a little organized obstruction) that he never applied for the Closure. [9] He had happily nothing to fear from the House of Lords, who still regarded the domain of Finance as

[7] " Harcourt ", II, 307–308.

[8] All the details are to be found in Appendix V of Gardiner's " Harcourt."

[9] Rather to the chagrin of some of his colleagues, who had important measures of their own in hand.

a preserved area, upon which they were forbidden to poach. In the result he covered himself with glory, some of which fell with a reflected and much-needed glow upon colleagues who were still engaged in " ploughing the sands."

Notwithstanding this conspicuous success, the position of the Government at the opening of the new session in 1895 was precarious in the extreme. The Parnellite members under Mr. John Redmond went over to the Opposition, and Harcourt wrote to the Queen that the " Government cannot count at most on a majority of more than fifteen." There was a Cabinet crisis in February, caused by Lord Rosebery's intimation of his intention to resign, on the ground that he was not sufficiently supported or defended by his colleagues. This blew over after a couple of days, with the paradoxical result that ostensibly friendly personal relations were reached between the Prime Minister and Harcourt, which were maintained until the downfall of the Administration. Moreover, in the early weeks of the session, there was a series of debating encounters, in each of which it was generally conceded that the honours rested with the spokesmen of the Government. The most remarkable performance was Fowler's [10] speech on the Indian cotton duties — by far his greatest parliamentary effort — which so discomfited the Opposition that the Government, for the first time in its history, had a three-figure majority — 304 to 109. Harcourt

[10] He had become Secretary of State for India, when Lord Kimberley went to the Foreign Office.

himself followed this up by an almost equally crushing dialectical triumph over his favourite victims — the Bimetallists. When the Easter holidays came he was able to write exultingly to Tom Ellis, who had become Chief Whip:

" But for you, I could never have got the vessel through such cramped waters. As it is, we have finished up with a blaze of triumph, and our insolent foes go chopfallen to eat their addled Easter eggs. So perish the ungodly! " [11]

A most characteristic outburst, which illustrates how, when he pleased, he could endear himself to those with whom he worked.

The strenuous business of the session was diversified by several lighter interludes: the election to the speakership of a distinguished lawyer, who had taken so modest a part in the business of the House, that both Harcourt and Balfour declared that they did not know him by sight; the claim put forward by three eldest sons of peers — Mr. G. Curzon, Lord Wolmer, and Mr. St. J. Brodrick, who were called the " Romeo Lords " — to continue (at their option) to sit in the House of Commons after the death of their fathers; and the proposal of the Government to erect a statue of Oliver Cromwell, which had a curious history [12] and strange consequences.

The chief legislative effort of this session was a measure which had a prominent place in the New-

[11] " Harcourt ", II, 359.
[12] It was withdrawn in consequence of an unholy combination between Mr. Balfour and the Nationalists.

258 FIFTY YEARS OF BRITISH PARLIAMENT

castle Programme — the Disestablishment of the
Welsh Church. The Bill was in my hands, and much
time and care had been expended upon its construction. The subject was one which raised countless
points of principle and policy, and which bristled
with technical difficulties. The Committee stage afforded as ample a scope as any Opposition could desire both for legitimate criticism and for obstructive
tactics. Sir Richard Temple in his " Story of My
Life " has given a graphic account of the organization of the campaign. The work was divided between
two sections: the " Corner Men " — of whom Sir
Richard himself was one — and the " Church Brigade ", which was officered by Sir Richard Webster
and Sir A. Griffith Boscawen. " At one time," says
Sir R. Temple, " we feared lest the speaking should
fall too much on a few individuals. I myself had
made twelve or more speeches in a few sittings, and
some of my comrades had done still more. So we
appealed to the ' Brigade '; fresh speakers reinforced
us, and very welcome they were." " After one night's
sitting, one line out of a bill many pages long, on
another night two lines, on another night three lines,
would be passed. The subject was a noble one, ad-
mitting of fine controversy. So we pressed many
points of history, of tradition, of finance, of topog-
raphy, into the service of our argument." [13]

The great guns of the Front Opposition Bench —
Mr. Balfour, Sir M. Hicks Beach, Mr. Goschen —
were frequently brought into action, and even Mr.

[13] " The Story of My Life ", Temple, II, 294–295.

Chamberlain, in the guise of an ardent Disestablisher, now and again peppered us with his cross-fire.

I had the valuable help of one of my Cabinet colleagues — Mr. Bryce; but my two regular lieutenants were Mr. George Russell, who was now Under-Secretary at the Home Office, and Sir Frank Lockwood, who had recently become Solicitor-General. George Russell had a pretty oratorical turn, but his talents were more suited to a full-dress debate than to the spade-work of Committee. Lockwood was one of my oldest and dearest friends both at the Bar and in politics, readiest of wits and most charming of companions, with a finer gift of caricature than any of his contemporaries, a favourite and effective advocate with a jury, and in every sense the best of good fellows. But neither of them was versed in the intricacies of ecclesiastical law and ecclesiastical finance. The Welsh members, well shepherded by their compatriot Tom Ellis, were naturally warm supporters of the principle of the Bill; but there were ardent spirits among them who thought that the process of what the " Church Brigade " called " spoliation and sacrilege " ought to have been handled by the Government in a more drastic fashion. One of the youngest of them, a natural *frondeur*, and already an acute and accomplished debater, Mr. Lloyd George, from time to time gave me a certain amount of trouble. I soon found that it was never safe to leave the Treasury Bench for more than a quarter of an hour, and after twelve days of Committee, in which little substantial progress had been made, and our majorities had ranged between eleven and seven, it was with a sigh of relief that, when the Government was defeated on another and wholly unexpected issue, I laid down my thankless task.

I was more fortunate with another Bill which passed into law: The Factories and Workshops Act of 1895. It was a comprehensive measure for extending and amending the law for the better security of the safety and health of workers — a subject which engaged my close and constant attention during the whole of my term at the Home Office. Its main provisions, which are too complicated and technical to form part of a general narrative, are summarized in an appendix at the end of this chapter.

Bills conceived in the same spirit to deal with the Regulation of Coal Mines and with the Truck System, together with measures of a more contentious character (Local Veto, Plural Voting, etc.) had not advanced beyond their early stages, when they were engulfed in the general cataclysm.

The cataclysm — if such it can be called — came without any premonitory rumblings on June 21. It was an " off " night, allocated to a subject which generally empties the House — the Army Estimates, which were in the safe hands of one of the most capable and quite the most popular of the members of the Cabinet — Mr. Campbell-Bannerman. By a felicitous mixture of firmness and tact he had just secured the resignation of the Duke of Cambridge of the post of Commander-in-chief which he had held for the best part of forty years. " No one except you," said Queen Victoria to her Minister, " could have managed it." Every one predicted a quiet evening; Members trooped off early to dinner; and Sir W. Harcourt, strolling on the Terrace, is reported to have said, " Thank Heaven! There is one night on which we need not fear a crisis." [14] Within an hour or two the crisis came. Campbell-Bannerman was charged by M. Brodrick with not having provided a sufficient reserve of cordite. His reply was that in the opinion of his expert advisers the reserve, which had been steadily increasing, was ample. He declined in the public interest to state the actual figures, but offered to show them to the Opposition leaders. Mr. Balfour, Mr. Chamberlain and Mr. Goschen nevertheless joined in the attack, and in a thin House the Opposition (supported in the Division Lobby by Sir Charles Dilke) carried their motion to reduce the salary of the Secretary of State by a majority of seven.

It was a " snap " division, which had been carefully engineered, and there is little doubt that the Government could, if they had been so minded, have had the decision reversed. But they had had enough of living from hand to mouth, and when the Cabinet met the only alternatives which they seriously considered were resignation and dissolution. The

[14] I remember that, after wrestling with a deputation of Welsh members, I got a " pair ", and went home to my wife, who was in her bedroom recovering from a tedious illness. She told me that she had just had successive and overlapping visits from Sir W. Harcourt and Mr. John Morley, each of whom chaffed the other on being found in such a place when the House was still sitting.

majority were at first unquestionably in favour of
dissolution, which I have never doubted was strategi-
cally the right course. But both Rosebery and Harcourt were strong for resignation, and the Cabinet
was so impressed by the unusual — the almost unprecedented — spectacle of their cordial agreement
with one another, that it deferred to their combined
authority, and Lord Rosebery proceeded to place his
and their offices at the disposal of the Queen.

Factories and Workshops Act, 1895

A well-informed summary of this Act is given by
Miss A. M. Anderson, Principal Lady Inspector of
Factories, in the " Encyclopædia Britannica ", tenth
edition, from which the following sentences are extracted.

Some of the provisions involved the introduction
of new principles, as in the prohibition of the use of
a dangerous machine or structure by the order of a
magistrate's court, and the power to include in the
special rules drawn up in pursuance of section 8 of
the Act of 1891, the prohibition of the employment
of any class of persons in any process scheduled by
order of the Secretary of State. . . . With the exercise of the latter power passed away, without opposition, the absolute freedom of the employer of the
adult male labourer to carry on his manufacture without legislative limitation of the hours of labour.
Second only in significance to these new developments was the addition for the first time since 1867,
of new classes of work places not covered by the
general definitions in section 93 of the Consolidating

Act of 1878, viz. (*a*) laundries (with special conditions as to hours, etc.); (*b*) docks, wharves, quays, warehouses and premises on which machinery worked by power is temporarily used for the purpose of the construction of a building or any structural work in connexion with the building (for the purpose only of obtaining security against accidents).

Other entirely new provisions . . . were the requirement of a reasonable temperature in workrooms, the requirement of lavatories for the use of persons employed in any department where poisonous substances are used, the obligation on occupiers and medical practitioners to report cases of industrial poisoning; and the penalties imposed on an employer wilfully allowing wearing apparel to be made, cleaned or repaired in a dwelling-house where an inmate is suffering from infectious disease. . . .

Other sections, relating to sanitation and safety, were developments of previous regulations rather than fresh departures, e.g. the fixing of a standard of overcrowding, provision of sanitary accommodation separate for each sex, where the standard of the Public Health Act Amendment Act of 1890 had not been adopted, power to order a fan or other mechanical means to carry off injurious gas, vapour or other impurity (the previous power covering only dust). Under the head of safety, the fencing of machinery and definition of accidents were made more precise, young persons were prohibited from cleaning dangerous machinery and additional safeguards against risk of injury by fire or panic were introduced.

On the question of employment the two foremost amendments lay in the almost complete prohibition of overtime for young persons and the restriction of the power of an employer to employ protected persons outside his factory or workshop on the same day that he had employed them in the factory or work-shop. Under the head of particulars of work and wages to pieceworkers an important and new power, highly valued by the workers, was given to apply the principle with the necessary modifications by order of the Secretary of State to industries other than textile.

CHAPTER XXXVIII

T HE general election of 1895 was the prelude to ten years of uninterrupted government by the now consolidated Unionists. Their term of power witnessed momentous changes both in the personnel of politics and in the fortunes of parties; the disappearance of Mr. Gladstone; the resignation of the Liberal leadership, first by Lord Rosebery, and then by Sir W. Harcourt; the break-up of the Liberal Party, and its reunion; the deaths, among the Liberal chiefs, of Kimberley and Harcourt, and among the Tories of Lord Salisbury himself; and, finally, the disintegration of the Unionists over the fiscal issue, which led to their crushing electoral disaster in January, 1906.

As in 1895–1896 we have reached, and passed, the end of the first twenty-five years in the period which is the subject of this review, it seems convenient, before we start on the second half of the general narrative, to call a halt for a spell of more or less desultory reminiscence.

So far, from 1868 to 1894, the dominating personality in parliamentary life had been that of Gladstone: the death of Lord Beaconsfield in 1881 removed his only rival; whether it would have been well for Gladstone's fame if he had died at the same time, on the morrow of his greatest personal triumph — the election of 1880 — will always be a problem for the historians; but it is beyond question that, during the fourteen years in which he still remained upon the battlefield, he was the solitary figure of heroic stature.

It is not beneath what used to be rather absurdly called the " Dignity of History " [1] to preserve the memory of the higher moods, and the casual and informal utterances, of great men. There is no more charming or illuminating chapter in Lord Morley's monumental biography than that in which he reports the talks of Gladstone when his harness was laid aside. I had not the privilege of anything like intimacy with him till the end of his life. But I have thought that some notes of conversations at which I was present may not be without interest, and may even help to fill in some details in the picture which Lord Morley has so deftly and so faithfully drawn. They are mostly taken from the diary to which I have already referred.

1891. December 12. Dined at Sir A. West's: Mr. and Mrs. Gladstone, Lord Carrington, J. Morley, Sir R. Welby and Self. Sat next Mr. Gladstone. Looks better than six months ago. No signs of feebleness or languor. Deaf with the left ear, but not with the right; conversation animated, rhetorical, and full of gesture.

It is just sixty years since he first visited Florence.

---

[1] A phrase which we owe to Bolingbroke and Fielding.

In those days, and up to the end, the Austrian Dominions in Italy were less oppressively governed than the Italian Duchies, Naples, the States of the Church, etc.

It was the cue of the Austrians to encourage misgovernment in these smaller States that they might profit by the contrast. Tuscany for this purpose may be regarded as Austrian. No great abuses in Lombardy and Venetia. Yet the Austrians were twice as much detested as any of the other Governments. The Italian saw and hated in the Hapsburgs the foreigner as well as the despot. The boycotting, not only of the Austrians, but of the Italians who took service under them, was complete and pitiless.

This subject (together with Ireland, which is always at the back of his mind, and moves easily and naturally to the front) led him to some general observations on the right of insurrection. The most striking was this: " Theologians and moralists forget that, when St. Paul counsels subjection to the powers that be, he is speaking of the individual as individual, and had not the case of communities in his view. I am persuaded that there is nothing more permanently demoralizing to a nation than passive acquiescence in unmerited suffering."

We talked of Rosebery's Pitt. Mr. Gladstone: " I am a Pittite up to 1793, but from that year to the end I am a Foxite out and out. . . . The period from 1783 to 1793 is unquestionably the most brilliant in the history of Parliament. Pitt, Fox, Sheridan, Burke, all of their best; and Lord North — a considerable speaker — still there for part of the time. On the Regency question in 1789 the Irish Parliament were undoubtedly right. They took up the logical and constitutional position, between the two extremes of Pitt on the one side and Fox on the other." Mr. Gladstone, naturally, differs altogether from Rosebery's apologetic view of Pitt's Irish policy. " Pitt never forgave the Irish their rejection of his deformed commercial proposals in 1785 (alluding to the resolution which would have made the Irish Parliament subordinate to the British in respect of Navigation Laws, etc.). Pitt thought better of Lord Fitzwilliam than Rosebery does. Else why should he have wished, near the end, to make him a Secretary of State? "

I asked him about the epidemic of suicide in the next political generation — Whitbread, Romilly, Castlereagh. He has no theory about it, but mentioned having heard the late Lord Derby say that Lord Althorp (" the best man beyond comparison in politics in my time ") told him that, between 1830–1834 (when he led the House of Commons) he had often felt, on getting up in the morning, that if there were a pair of loaded pistols by his bedside, he would, without hesitation, blow out his brains.

" The three men of the greatest Parliamentary courage I have known were Peel, Lord John Russell, and Disraeli. Disraeli had the most. The only man who could write Disraeli's life properly is the present (the 15th) Lord Derby. Disraeli thought more of him, and was more intimate with him, than any other colleague. The hardest task I ever had to discharge was the delivery of an *éloge* on Disraeli in the House of Commons after his death."

Carrington spoke of the famous Bucks election in 1876, in the midst of the Bulgarian agitation, when his brother Rupert was beaten by Fremantle. Lord Granville wrote Rupert's election address. The Prince of Wales, ignorant of this and suspecting Rosebery to be the author, told Granville that he thought it " wretched bosh." Mr. Gladstone: " It was the

most momentous bye-election in my time in this sense
— that, if it had gone the other way, it would have
reversed the whole policy of England. One hundred
and seventy-one clergymen voted and turned the
election; only two of the number voted for Carrington, one of whom I personally canvassed."

He spoke of Sir G. Cornewall Lewis, of whom he
has the highest opinion, though they never agreed on
finance. He was a lazy and bad administrator, but
" one of the best and most sagacious men I have ever
known in Council "; not a good speaker, but with a
dry humour, and a particular favourite of the House
of Commons. A really great scholar of the erudite,
not elegant, type; the " Astronomy of the Ancients "
his worst book.

In reference to recent discussions about the House
of Lords setting the House of Commons right, or in-
sisting on reference of new policy to the people, Mr.
Gladstone instanced the Ecclesiastical Titles Bill —
fought strenuously for four months by a small minority in the Commons, and then went through the
House of Lords " like a shot."

He spoke of A. J. Balfour, as he knew him twenty
years ago, before he went into politics; he was then
very attractive and candid, with a great dialectical
gift, and not a Tory either in conviction or sentiment.
Has since much deteriorated!

After dinner talked for a time with Mrs. G. about
my domestic affairs and her own trouble.[2] Very kind
and natural. She has been harder hit than he, or
shows it more. Mr. G. came up and said he wanted to
speak to me for a few minutes. She left us, and he
at once plunged into Home Rule, with especial reference to my appeal for some more explicit statement
of what he means to propose.

[2] The recent death of their eldest son.

He is not indisposed to satisfy honest and reasonable curiosity, but unwilling to enlarge the enemy's field of criticism, or to fetter himself by pledges. I specified as examples — not as exhausting the case: (1) retention of Irish members; (2) assuming retention, their voting powers — on all subjects, or only on some? (I spoke strongly for former, and he *seemed* to agree); (3) future of Irish police; (4) Irish judiciary. He added, smiling, " the Irish Peers." He spoke vehemently about Michelstown, Kinsella's case, etc., as having increased to impossibility the difficulty of handing over the present Constabulary to a Home Rule Government.

I told him what John O'Connor (" Long John "), a Parnellite, had said to me a few days ago; that the recent Irish elections had been won, not by Dillon & Co., nor by the priests, but in his (Mr. G.'s) name, and because the Irish electors were determined to give him the chance of settling the question. Mr. G. replied that, substituting the " Liberal party " for himself, this was probably true.

1892. March 15. Met Mr. G. at dinner at Lady Lyttelton's. Most interesting things I heard him say were about Sir James Graham and Peel. Graham came into Parliament in 1818 and was a failure; retired and spent eight years at Netherby, studying history and politics; came back to House of Commons about 1828, and was put in 1830 into Lord Grey's Cabinet, where he made a great reputation as administrator at the Admiralty. Never popular; too incisive,[3] but a good speaker.

In 1832, when I came in, Stanley (afterwards Lord Derby) was the favourite speaker on the Government

[3] Disraeli once said of him in the House that he " mistook insolence for invective."

side, and had most hold of the House. After a good speech from Peel, Parker, Liberal member for Sheffield, walking home with me, said: " Your Cock will soon be a good match for ours." (Meaning Stanley.)

The following is, perhaps, worth recording, as illustrating the variety of his topics:

1892. April 1. Dined at the Hayters'. Mr. G. there. He gave us some of his reminiscences of preachers: Dr. Chalmers, R. Hill, Edward Irving; spoke most highly of the last, but not a popular style. In a lull at dinner, I heard him dwelling, with much unction and in his best Parliamentary manner, to Arthur Cecil, the actor, on the immense and gratifying strides taken in his time by the art of Dentistry!

" Mr. Gladstone," Cardinal Manning is reported to have said, " is a substantive who likes to be attended by adjectives, and I am not exactly an adjective." A very superficial judgment. It was far from being true of him in politics, and still less so in social life, where he was not only a model of courtesy and fine manners, but always ready to give and take on even terms, subject to the natural advantage that Providence had endowed him with all the gifts of a great actor, not excluding (as some foolish people imagined) an excellent sense of humour.

The social stringency which was one of the features of the strained political situation in 1886 gradually relaxed, and I cannot recall a time when the social life of London was easier or more agreeably mixed. It became the fashion in the summer evenings to give dinners at the House of Commons, where, though the rooms were small and noisy, and the fare not always of the best, the Terrace, on a starlit night, was a favourite lounge for the wit and beauty of all parties; and often proved more attractive, and, except in the interludes occasioned by the Division bell, more crowded, than the green benches of the House.

During these years, Mr. Haldane and I used to give an annual dinner, on an " off night " in June or July, at the Blue Posts in Cork Street, where the cuisine (though simple) and the wine were seriously attended to. Regular guests were Rosebery, John Morley, George Meredith, Charles Bowen, and Arthur Balfour. Others, who came from time to time, were R. Churchill, Lowell (then American Minister in London), Lord Dufferin, Chamberlain, Sir Alfred Lyall, Burne-Jones, Edward Grey, George Curzon, Birrell, Harry Cust, Herbert Paul. I regret that I made no record of our conversations; but the best table talk has a bouquet which cannot be preserved. Meredith at his best was difficult to beat, and Bowen had a nimbleness of wit and finesse of phrase which were entirely his own. Among the politicians it would not have been easy to find two more accomplished masters of the nuances of conversation than Balfour and Morley.

CHAPTER XXXIX

LORD SALISBURY'S third Cabinet consisted of nineteen members — of whom fifteen (including Mr. Goschen) were Conservatives, and four were Liberal Unionists. The protracted liaison had at length become a legal union, and though the term " Liberal Unionist " survived for some years, it soon ceased to have anything more than an historical significance. Not a few of the party so named were men of great personal and parliamentary weight, and two — Devonshire and Chamberlain — of marked individuality. Yet, like the Peelites of an earlier generation, they succumbed to what was then regarded in British politics as a law of Nature — the two-party system; the Irish Nationalists had always been regarded as a temporary excrescence which, in turn, when it served its immediate purpose, was destined to be absorbed.[1]

The fusion placed at Lord Salisbury's disposal, in the formation of his new Administration, an almost embarrassing wealth of talent and capacity. Goschen, who had now joined the Carlton Club, was trans-

---

[1] Sir W. Harcourt's description of the Unionist fusion is characteristic. " The cremation of Liberal-Unionism has at last been performed in the Tory Crematory. Peace to their ashes! There is one imposture less in the world."

ferred at his own request to the Admiralty from the
Exchequer, which was entrusted to Hicks Beach.
The other wing of the consolidated party was generously provided for. The Duke of Devonshire became President of the Council; the Colonial Office
was given to Mr. Chamberlain, and the War Office
to Lord Lansdowne; and Sir Henry James (created
Lord James of Hereford) entered the Cabinet as
Chancellor of the Duchy.

I have not hitherto had occasion to make more
than a passing reference to Henry James. He had
been for many years a conspicuous figure both at the
Bar and in the House of Commons. He rose to the
head of his profession, where his reputation was that,
not of a profound lawyer, but of an exceptionally
dexterous and persuasive advocate. He was Attorney-General from 1880 to 1885. Mr. Gladstone held
him in high estimation, and in the course of those
years thought of him twice at critical moments, once
for the speakership, and again for the office of Chief
Secretary for Ireland. If he could have seen his way
(as some people did) to get over or round one or two
anti-Home Rule speeches which he had made during
the general election of 1885, he would have been
Lord Chancellor in the Gladstone Government of
1886. He then attached himself to the Hartington
section of the Liberal Unionists, but never for a
moment lost the good will of his old political friends.
With Harcourt in particular (whose " best man " he
had been at his second marriage) he maintained to
the end the most cordial relations. In reply to a letter

of congratulation from James on his leadership of the
Opposition during the Session of 1896, Harcourt
writes: " There is nothing in the world like old
friends and old wine, and you are my choicest bin." [2]
I belonged, of course, to a later generation, but by a
happy accident I was brought into contact with him
while I was still a young and struggling barrister, and
he was already Attorney-General. I " devilled " for
him for some years, and it was largely owing to his
unfailing kindness and partiality that I found my
feet at the Bar. I have never known a truer friend, or
a man of better heart or more unbounded generosity.
When, in 1903, the fiscal controversy was started by
Chamberlain, James, who had all his life been a
convinced and ardent Free Trader, broke with his
Unionist associates, and, though now disabled by age
and illness from active political warfare, was once
more heart and soul with his old party.

The new Cabinet had an overwhelmingly successful début at the general election of 1895. The
Unionists (Conservative and Liberal combined)
numbered 411 in the House of Commons, as against
an Opposition of not more than 259 (Liberals 177,
Nationalists 82). As the Government had the House
of Lords completely under their control, their position
appeared to be, and in fact was, one of unassailable
strength. More remarkable even than the changes in
the comparative aggregates were the personal disasters which befell the most eminent of the Liberal
leaders. Both Harcourt and Morley lost their Eng-

[2] " Harcourt ", II, 410.

lish seats and had to take refuge in Wales and Scotland, which had remained relatively faithful to the party.[3] " We must send politics to the devil for six months at least," wrote " C.-B." on the eve of his annual departure for Marienbad.

Harcourt, who was never cast down by disaster, wrote to me (July 29): " As survivors of the shipwrecked crew, we shall have to set to work, I suppose, to set up a Robinson Crusoe habitation of some sort about the 12th. I was prepared for the deluge but not for this earthquake. However, we must put the boldest face on it we can."

It is not necessary to write more than two or three sentences of the legislative work of 1896–1897. Bills for the relief of the landed interest from the burden of agricultural rates, and for buttressing up the finance of voluntary schools passed into law. The opposition to them, as was acknowledged by both friends and foes, was brilliantly led by Sir W. Harcourt. A less controversial and more beneficent measure was the Workmen's Compensation Act, which was due to the inspiration of Mr. Chamberlain.

Meanwhile the superficial tranquillity of the domestic situation was disturbed from quarters so diverse and remote as Armenia and South Africa.

A series of massacres in the Armenian provinces of Turkey, of the usual type, but on an exceptional scale, aroused deep popular indignation in Great

[3] Campbell-Bannerman and I, who were Scottish Members, both improved our position at the polls.

Britain. Lord Salisbury addressed solemn warnings to the Sultan; the Ambassadors of the Great Powers at Constantinople made their traditional protests; but it soon became evident that Russia and other Powers were opposed to coercive action. The question at once arose: should Great Britain alone intervene, and, if necessary, by force? Mr. Gladstone, in the last public speech of his life, made at Liverpool on September 24, 1896, did not hesitate to answer the question in the affirmative. The fervour of the old Bulgarian days once more glowed in his veins. " Had I," he said to one of his sons, " the years of 1876 upon me, gladly would I start another campaign, even if as long as that." [4]

A large and important section of his old followers was aroused by his appeal, and ready to follow his lead. But the bulk of the Liberal Party, though not satisfied with Lord Salisbury's paper protests, were not prepared to urge action which might land Europe in war. Sir William Harcourt (as might be expected) was strongly of this opinion.

So also was Lord Rosebery, and to the surprise of the world and the consternation of his followers, he seized this opportunity formally to lay down the leadership of the party. On October 8, in a letter composed and published without consultation with any of his old colleagues, and addressed to the Chief Whip, Mr. T. Ellis, he wrote:

[4] It may be recalled that it was in reference to this particular phase of the Eastern Question that Lord Salisbury — speaking of both political parties — used the memorable expression, " that we had put our money on the wrong horse." (House of Lords, January 19, 1897.)

The recent course of events makes it necessary to clear the air. I find myself in apparent difference with a considerable mass of the Liberal Party on the Eastern Question, and in some conflict of opinion with Mr. Gladstone, who must necessarily always exercise a matchless authority in the Party, while scarcely from any quarter do I receive explicit support. . . . This situation, except as regards Mr. Gladstone, is not altogether new.

His speech the following day, October 9, at a meeting at Edinburgh at which, amongst others, Fowler and I were present, did not carry the matter much further; except that it indicated pretty clearly his opinion that the inherent difficulties in the position of a Liberal leader, who is also a peer, called for exceptional loyalty and coöperation from the party inside and outside, and that such exceptional treatment had not been accorded to him.

Lord Morley, writing many years after, makes the following comments on Lord Rosebery's letter of resignation: [5]

The language was guarded, and what by diplomatists is called correct. But personal implications are not easy in the popular eye to dissemble. A political party, strange as this may seem, is at the same time both the roughest, and one of the most delicate, of human machines. Ever so slight a new personal element suffices at the shortest notice to awaken suspicions, pretences, exclusions, exaggeration, bits of small malice, all multiplied daily and swollen in geometric progression by gossip. In this

[5] " Recollections ", II, 82.

case personal partialities were undoubtedly identified with honest differences of political leaning. It needs no great knowledge either of English politics, or of the heart of man, to realize the murky atmosphere in which the Liberal leaders had now to work.

" The murky atmosphere " had, in point of fact — notwithstanding honest and strenuous efforts, by myself amongst others, to disperse it — been brooding and hovering over the scene for more than a year. The final resignation had been preceded by many premonitory signs, and ought not perhaps to have surprised some of us as much as it did. One or two contemporary comments of Lord Rosebery's late colleagues are worth recording:

RIPON to ROSEBERY: " You have handed us over to Harcourt without escape, and you are not ignorant of all which that means."

KIMBERLEY to RIPON: " In all the circumstances I am not disposed to be angry with R. for seizing an opportunity to get out of an intolerable situation." [6]

CAMPBELL-BANNERMAN frankly said that greatly as he deplored, he was not surprised at Lord R.'s decision. [7]

More interesting, perhaps, than any of these are the dicta of Harcourt himself, from the " safe retreat of Malwood " :

HARCOURT to LORD RUSSELL L.C.J.: " You will find us here in the midst of a very unintelligible per-

[6] " Life of Ripon ", II, 246–247.   [7] Spender's " Life ", I, 185.

turbation, owing to Rosebery's resignation, the cause
and object of which I am wholly at a loss to understand. I hate all rows and most of all personal rows.
. . . I always think what a wise man Reynolds was:

> " ' When they talked of their Raphaels, Correggios
>   and stuff,
> He shifted his trumpet and only took snuff.'

" I should like a pinch out of your box." [8]

HARCOURT to MORLEY: . . . " For my part I
really do not see what is changed, except that there is
a Liberal the less. Of course the reasons given by
Rosebery for bolting are not the true ones. It was
neither Mr. G. nor our humble selves, his colleagues.
I believe he funked the future which he saw before
him — that he felt called upon to say something on
politics in general and give a lead, and that he did
not know what to say, and so took up his hat and
departed." [9]

HARCOURT to MORLEY (later): " The idiots in the
Press seem to think every one is ready to cut one
another's throat in order to become ' Leader of the
Liberal Party.' For my part, if I did not think it
currish to bolt in the presence of difficulties, I should
take up my hat and say good-bye." [10]

---

[8] " Harcourt ", II, 418.

[9] *Ibid.*

[10] As I was myself supposed to be one of these wholly imaginary
candidates, I may be allowed to quote from another letter (Harcourt to
Morley, November 4): "Every effort has been made by the mischief-
makers to cause ill blood between me and Asquith, but I have steadily
refused to listen to them. I have had every reason to rely on his good
faith and goodwill, and never allow myself to be influenced by gossip."

The only formal change made in consequence of Lord Rosebery's resignation was the election by a meeting of Liberal peers in January, 1897, of Lord Kimberley to be their leader in the House of Lords. Sir W. Harcourt continued to lead in the House of Commons.

CHAPTER XL

THE RAID — AND AFTER

T HE current of domestic affairs was again coloured and deflected from South Africa. The Boers in the course of their wanderings had been unlucky enough — in defiance of all geological probabilities — first to stumble upon a diamond field, and then upon a gold reef. The Transvaal, where they might reasonably have expected to find for themselves and their flocks and herds the tranquil seclusion of a pastoral life, was invaded by a cosmopolitan crowd of diggers with its inevitable train of speculators and adventurers. Cecil Rhodes, who had become Prime Minister of the Cape Colony, was sincerely anxious for a harmonious concordat between the Dutch and English elements throughout South Africa, but on terms which would secure union up to the Zambesi, with Britain as the predominant partner. The policy which for some years he skilfully and successfully pursued cannot be better described than in Mr. Spender's words.[1]

The North, in Mr. Rhodes' view, had to be British. If the Dutch got it they would prevent the British from following, set up hostile tariffs, bar the railways, and prevent the flow of trade on which the southern

[1] " Life of Campbell-Bannerman ", I, 188–189.

colonies depended. This was a shrewd and sound idea, which was no sooner conceived than acted upon with energy and courage. It required that Kruger should be anticipated in the North and shut out from the West or from any region where he could stride across the road from the Cape to the North. Up to 1895 Kruger had lost, and Rhodes won, every point in the game. The North was secured for the Chartered Company, Bechuanaland was annexed by the Imperial Government, the forlorn treks and spasmodic raids by which the Boers attempted to anticipate or overtake their unsleeping rival without exception headed off or turned back. The understanding between England and Portugal, and the 1884 Convention, cut them off from the sea on the East, and by letting the Swaziland Convention expire, they had missed their one opportunity of getting a port with the consent of Great Britain. History, in fact, could show no better example of skilful and business-like imperialism than British enterprise during the half-dozen years which ended in 1895.

The new situation brought about by the new immigration of the gold-hunters on the Rand put a check to the quiet and progressive development of Rhodes' scheme. There was constant and growing friction between the old Burgher oligarchy and the " Outlanders." The new industry was a source of great profit to the Boer Government, but they steadily refused to those engaged in it any voice or share in legislation or administration. The result was that the Outlanders, who had solid grievances which called for drastic measures of redress, finding protest and agitation ineffectual, began to organize a " bloodless revolution." They suffered from the lack of capable leadership, and were even much divided among themselves on what might seem a fundamental issue — whether they should raise the British flag, or become an independent Republican State. Mr. Rhodes, who was in full sympathy with their hostility to Krugerism, though sceptical as to the practicability of their methods, was kept informed (in his capacity of head of the Chartered Company) of what was going on, but was careful (in his other capacity of Prime Minister of the Cape Colony) to conceal what he knew from Sir Hercules Robinson, who was both Governor of the Cape and High Commissioner for South Africa. It seems clear that it was without any knowledge or privity on Rhodes' part that on December 31, 1895, Doctor Jameson, with five hundred of the Company's troopers, whom the Imperial Government had allowed for quite sufficient reasons to be mustered on the Bechuanaland border, made his famous raid into the Transvaal. An adventure more childishly conceived or more clumsily executed it is impossible to imagine, and it resulted in immediate and ignominious failure. Doctor Jameson and his fellow filibusters (together with their secret cipher) were captured by the Boers. They were handed over, with perhaps superfluous magnanimity, by President Kruger to the Imperial authorities, and having done by their blundering folly as great a disservice as it was possible to render, not only to the Outlanders, but to the best interests of the Empire, were, on their arrival in England, acclaimed and fêted by a section

of London society as the worthy successors of Drake
and Raleigh.

The new Poet Laureate, Alfred Austin, a lineal
descendant, in the poetic pedigree, of Eusden and
Pye, celebrated their exploits in some verses of sentimental doggerel, in the course of which he suggested
that one of the aims which inspired these modern
paladins was to rescue the honour of the English-
women in Johannesburg from the sinister designs of
the Boers.[2]

The Kaiser intervened with the famous telegram
to President Kruger, in which he congratulated the
Boers on their success in maintaining their independence against " foreign aggression " " without
appealing to the help of friendly Powers." [3] The international situation was, indeed, at the moment, as
Mr. Goschen, the inventor, or at any rate the popu-
larizer, of the phrase " splendid isolation " [4], wrote to
Lord Salisbury, " very bad in many directions." On
points, some of real and others of imaginary importance, there was diplomatic friction between Great
Britain and Germany, France, Russia, Turkey, and
even (over the Venezuelan Question) the United
States of America. Our isolation was (as Mr.

[2] " Jameson's Ride." — The *Times*, January 11, 1896.
" There are girls in the gold-reef city,
    There are mothers and children too!
And they cry, Hurry up! for pity!
    So what can a brave man do? "

[3] As to the actual authorship of this message, *see* " The Genesis of
the War ", pp. 12–13.
[4] " Life of Goschen ", II, 204. The phrase seems to have been first
used by the Canadian statesman, Mr. Foster.

Goschen boasted in a public speech) " not an isolation of weakness, but deliberately chosen." It had,
however, its inconveniences.

Nothing could have been more prompt or correct
than the steps at once taken by Mr. Chamberlain, the
Colonial Secretary. His condemnation of the raid
was severe and uncompromising. He communicated
his more important dispatches, before sending them,
to his Liberal predecessor, Lord Ripon, and both
Lord Rosebery and Sir William Harcourt paid public
tributes to the admirable manner in which he had
handled the situation.

Doctor Jameson and his associates were put on
their trial in London, and received what were generally regarded as inadequate sentences. Upon this
point there is much force in what Lord George Hamilton, who was a member of the Government at the
time, has written in his Reminiscences (1886–
1906).[5]

In my judgment the punishment inflicted upon the
officers concerned was quite insufficient. They should
have been simultaneously cashiered. As it was, most
of them, after their temporary punishment, crept
back into the Army. . . . These light sentences and
the approval shown in certain social circles, of the
offenders, did us, as a nation and Government, incalculable harm. It was another illustration of
" Albion's perfidy ", and the prejudice and hostility
shown towards us by the world at large when, later
on, we were obliged to accept Kruger's challenge, can
be traced to a legitimate resentment against not

[5] P. 287.

merely the outrageous nature of the offence, but the
highly inadequate sentences inflicted upon the promoters."

The cipher telegrams which the raiders had left
behind them on the field of Doornkop, having been
in due course published at Pretoria, abundantly
proved the complicity of Mr. Rhodes and his Company in the proposed insurrection (though not in the
raid itself) and naturally led to urgent demands for
a full public inquiry. A select committee of the House
of Commons was accordingly appointed and sat from
February to July, 1897. Its members included Mr.
Chamberlain himself, Sir W. Harcourt and Sir H.
Campbell-Bannerman; and among the witnesses was
Mr. Rhodes, who had by this time resigned his office
as Prime Minister of the Cape and his directorship of
the Chartered Company. It is unnecessary here to
rehearse the proceedings of the committee, which are
fully and lucidly described both by Mr. Gardiner and
Mr. Spencer in their biographies. Its report, drafted
in substance by Harcourt and accepted by Chamberlain, was a unanimous and unmeasured condemnation
of the conduct of Mr. Rhodes.

There was a good deal that was open to criticism
in some parts of the procedure of the committee; in
particular, its failure to compel the production of the
" Hawksley " telegrams. This gave rise to an absurd
suspicion, which was current for years, that, in order
to shield the Colonial Office, there had been a pact of
secrecy between the two Front Benches. Still more

unfortunate was Mr. Chamberlain's declaration, in the final debate in the House of Commons, that nothing had been proved to affect Mr. Rhodes' " personal position as a man of honour." In the narrower sense, in which dishonour implies illicit pecuniary gain, this was perfectly true, but in the larger and fuller sense it was at least difficult to reconcile with the findings of the report.

CHAPTER XLI

1898

IN the year 1898 the attention of Parliament was largely given to extraneous affairs in different quarters of the world; the controversy with President Cleveland over the Venezuelan boundary; the retention on the Indian frontier of the small State of Chitral, with the maintenance of a military road to it through the territory of independent tribes; the war between Turkey and Greece which resulted in the autonomy of Crete; and the advantage taken by the Powers of the paralysis of China — Kiao-Chow and valuable mining rights in Shantung falling to Germany, and Port Arthur, with an ice-free outlet to the Pacific (despite British protests) to Russia. By way of consolation or set-off, we obtained a lease of Wei-hai-wei.

Lord Salisbury was a cautious Foreign Minister, of the " large map " school, with no predisposition to a Forward policy, and on the whole (like Mr. Goschen) in no way anxious that Great Britain should abandon her attitude of " splendid isolation." The mantle of Lord Beaconsfield had never fitted him, but few would have predicted that the new Elisha was to come from Birmingham. In the hectic days of Jingoism Mr. Chamberlain had boasted that he was a " parochial " statesman, and had warned his fellow countrymen that " already (i.e. in 1878) the weary Titan staggers under the too vast orb of her fate."

He had now become a convinced Expansionist, and the advocate of a policy of alliances. Speaking at Birmingham in May, 1898, he struck the keynote of his new diplomacy, taking as his text the cession of Port Arthur to Russia, and the methods by which it had been brought about. (" Who sups with the devil must have a long spoon.") He urged the maintenance of " bonds of permanent amity " with the United States. The " bonds " contemplated were not to be of a merely sentimental, or even material, character. " Terrible as war might be, even war itself would be cheaply purchased if, in a great and noble cause, the Stars and Stripes and the Union Jack should wave together over an Anglo-Saxon Alliance." But his real objective was an Alliance against Russia.

" It is impossible," he said, " to overrate the gravity of the issue. It is not a question of a single port in China — that is a very small matter. It is not the question of a single province. It is a question of the whole fate of the Chinese Empire, and our interests in China are so great, our proportion of the trade so enormous and the potentialities of that trade so gigantic, that I feel no more vital question has ever been presented for the decision of a Government and the decision of a nation. . . . If the policy of isolation, which has hitherto been the policy of this country, is to be maintained in the future, then the fate of the Chinese Empire may be, probably will be, hereafter decided without reference to our wishes and in defiance of our interests. If, on the other hand, we are determined to enforce the policy of the open door, to preserve an equal opportunity for trade with all our rivals, then we must not allow Jingoes to drive us into a quarrel with all the world at the same time, and we must not reject the idea of an alliance with those Powers whose interests most nearly approximate to our own."

This speech naturally created an uneasy impression, and, it would seem, caused some embarrassment to Lord Salisbury,[1] who, however, declined to express any opinion upon it in the House of Lords. On the Foreign Office Vote in the House of Commons,[2] I took the opportunity to express the prevailing view in the Liberal Party.

If hostility to Russia was to be the end of our foreign policy, was an alliance, I asked, with some unknown, some unnamed, power to be the means?

"What have we done? What have the people of Great Britain done or suffered that, after bearing, as we have borne for over fifty years, the ever-growing weight of empire on our own unaided shoulders, and borne it without finding the burden too heavy for the courage, enterprise and self-reliance of our people — what have we done or suffered that we are now to go touting for allies in the highways and byways of Europe? "

[1] "Life of Goschen ", II, 220.   [2] June 10, 1898.

Mr. Chamberlain replied that he did not advise an alliance any more than he rejected it; he had only pointed out the consequences of rejecting it, and the advantages which might result from accepting it. " I have not resigned; I am not cast out by my colleagues; I am not rejected by the Prime Minister."

Later on in the year, speaking at Manchester in November, 1898, Mr. Chamberlain indicated what he meant by " alliances ", France, this time, being selected as the potential enemy. It was just after the affair at Fashoda. The people of this country, he said, wanted to be friends of the great nation on the other side of the Channel, but he complained that in Egypt, Newfoundland, West Africa, Madagascar, and elsewhere throughout the world, French influence had been exerted without regard to British susceptibilities and interests. On the following day he advocated closer relations with Germany as well as a combination between the two great English-speaking peoples.

Finally a year later (November 30, 1899) in the early stages of the Boer War, Mr. Chamberlain developed his policy, fully fledged, in a speech at Leicester:

" There is something more which I think any far-seeing English statesman must have long desired, and that is that we should not remain permanently isolated on the continent of Europe, and I think that the moment that aspiration was formed it must have appeared evident to everybody that the natural alliance was between ourselves and the great German

Empire. We have had our differences with Germany, we have had our quarrels and contentions, we have had our misunderstandings. I do not conceal that the people of this country have been irritated, and justly irritated, by circumstances which we are only too glad to forget, but at the root of things there has been a force which has necessarily brought us together. What, then, unites nations? Interest and sentiment. What interest have we which is contrary to the interest of Germany?

" I cannot conceive any point which can arise in the immediate future which would bring ourselves and the Germans into antagonism of interests. On the contrary, I can see many things which must be a cause of anxiety to the statesmen of Europe, but in which our interests are clearly the same as the interests of Germany and in which that understanding of which I have spoken in the case of America might, if extended to Germany, do more, perhaps, than any combination of arms in order to preserve the peace of the world.

" If the union between England and America is a powerful factor in the cause of peace, a new Triple Alliance between the Teutonic race and the two branches of the Anglo-Saxon race will be a still more potent influence in the future of the world. I have used the word ' alliance ' . . . but again I desire to make it clear that to me it seems to matter little whether you have an alliance which is committed to paper, or whether you have an understanding in the minds of the statesmen of the respective countries.

An understanding is perhaps better than an alliance, which may stereotype arrangements which cannot be regarded as permanent in view of the changing circumstances from day to day."

These declarations (as we now know) were made after consultations at Windsor with Count Bülow (then German Foreign Secretary) who had accompanied the Kaiser on a visit there, and upon his assurance that he would reciprocate them in Berlin. But they were ill-received here, made a still worse impression in Germany, and were, in fact, repudiated (on December 11) in the Reichstag by Bülow in a speech which contained the memorable and significant sentence: " In the new century, Germany must be either the hammer or the anvil." Mr. Chamberlain came to the conclusion that " it was a bad job to try to do business with Berlin " and never renewed his overtures.[3]

[3] The history of this affair is given in " The Genesis of the War ", pp. 22–26.

CHAPTER XLII

A CHANGE OF LEADERSHIP
1898–1899

THE war in the Sudan, begun tentatively in 1896
by an advance to Dongola to check the Dervish
menace to Egypt, was brought to a successful conclusion in September, 1898, by the destruction of the
Khalifa's power at the battle of Omdurman, and the
hoisting of the British and Egyptian flags on the
palace at Khartoum. Within a month a French expedition, which had for some time been on its way
from the Congo to the Upper Nile, took possession of
Fashoda and an international situation of the utmost
delicacy was created. Thanks to the tact of Lord
Kitchener, and the dexterous diplomacy of Lord
Salisbury, the threatening danger was averted.

Harcourt, though he made no complaints, and had
no reason to complain, of lack of loyalty and support from his colleagues in the House of Commons,
was out of sympathy with many of them, and of the
party outside, in regard to the Sudanese affair, which
he regarded as another illustration of the mischiefs
of a Forward policy. His growing discontent with his
position (which he had persuaded himself was being
undermined by a " Rosebery intrigue ") came to a

head [1] early in December, 1898, when, in a letter to Mr. John Morley dated December 8, and published December 14, he announced his resignation of the leadership of the party in the House of Commons.[2] It seems that he had discussed the matter privately with Mr. Morley, but to the rest of his colleagues the letter was a complete surprise.

A party, he wrote, rent by sectional disputes and personal interests is one which no man can consent to lead either with credit to himself or advantage to the country. He could not consent to be a candidate for any contested position, and in arriving at the conclusion that he could best discharge his duty to the party in an independent position, he felt sure Mr. Morley would agree that a disputed leadership beset by distracted sections and conflicting interests is an impossible situation.

Mr. Morley replied in a letter sympathizing with, and approving of, Sir William Harcourt's decision. It contained some rhetorical passages which were read with open-eyed astonishment by the colleagues of both. One specimen will suffice: " There is something odious in telling a man who has stuck manfully to the ship instead of keeping snug in harbour because seas were rough and skies dark, that his position in his party is to be incessantly made matter of formal contest and personal challenge."

[1] In a letter to Mr. S. Buxton (January 4, 1899), Lord Ripon states that the immediate cause for the action taken by Harcourt was a speech on foreign policy by Sir E. Grey. *Sed quaere:* " Ripon's Life ", II, 251.
[2] Set out in full, " Harcourt ", II, 472.

Mr. Morley's letter was generally interpreted as meaning that he had resolved to share Harcourt's retirement. It is more than doubtful whether that was his intention at the time he wrote it. But a month later (January 17, 1899), speaking to his constituents at Brechin, after enlarging on the " dangerous doctrines " in foreign policy which were spreading even through the Liberal Party, he declared that he had come, independently of Harcourt's resignation, though substantially for the same reasons, to the conclusion that " he could not longer take an active and responsible part in the formal councils of the heads of the party."

Perhaps the best comment on these singular transactions is that of Sir H. Campbell-Bannerman, who (if anybody) was free from the faintest suspicion either of an intriguing temperament or of an " Imperialistic " bias. He writes to Sir Ralph Knox (January 2, 1899): [3]

This (a cold) had given me plenty of time to read, re-read, and study, two famous letters published recently, which have greatly perturbed our side of the House of Commons. I still do not know what it means. Who is it that has been intriguing, and against whom? Since a certain gentleman reproved sin, and two other gentlemen at Rome complained of sedition, we have seen nothing like it.

And a few days later (January 6) [4] he writes to Lord Rosebery:

[3] Spender, " Biography of Sir Henry Campbell-Bannerman ", I, 216.
[4] *Ibid.*, I, 217.

I pass over the letters themselves, as to which all of us who are acquainted with the facts cannot have two opinions. . . . Our people resent having been left to drift; and they are sick of the conception of public life which consists merely in their being expected to form an occasional ring, while some notable bruiser displays his science.

That there was at this time a real cleavage of opinion in the Liberal Party, which the South African situation developed, on important issues of policy, is beyond contradiction; that the unhappy personal relations between some of the leaders tended to widen and advertise the breach is equally certain; but there was no justification for the misleading impression, naturally and necessarily created by the Harcourt-Morley correspondence, that, either then or thereafter, those concerned were poisoned by the spirit, or tempted to resort to the methods, of dishonourable intrigue.

The " formal councils " of the Liberal Party in the House of Commons were, of course, seriously attenuated by the secession of Harcourt and Morley; indeed, there were only left in them four members of the late Cabinet: Campbell-Bannerman, Fowler, Bryce, and myself. Happily, there was no difference of opinion among the other three that Campbell-Bannerman should be invited to take the lead. The position offered no attraction to him. As he wrote to Lord Rosebery in a letter already quoted: " If I receive what in Kirk Sessions we style a ' call ', I am son enough of my country to do my best. I say this disregarding the fact that ordinary difficulties will be mightily increased by the existence of a pair of intellectuals sitting round the corner always ready to pounce. I know this well, but I think that it will be at once safest and most self-respecting for us who are to be responsible for the party to disregard them, and presume on their good behaviour, until they show that our confidence is misplaced." The " call " came, when at a meeting of Liberal members at the Reform Club — February 6, 1899 — " C.-B." was unanimously, and in a temper in which relief and enthusiasm were curiously blended, requested to undertake the leadership of the Liberal Party in the House of Commons. In the admirable speech[5] in which he accepted the invitation, he described himself as " well known to be a person of a pretty tolerant and easy-going disposition." He was that, but also a great deal more. I may be allowed to repeat here what I have said before; for no one had fuller opportunities than I had, sometimes in disagreement, far more often in complete and cordial agreement, of testing his qualities both of head and heart: " His was by no means the simple personality which many people supposed; it had its complexities and apparent incongruities, and even to those who were most intimate with him, sometimes its baffling features. But of all the men with whom I have been associated in public life, I put him as high as any in sense of duty, and in both moral and intellectual courage."[6]

[5] " Campbell-Bannerman ", I, 220–221.
[6] " Studies and Sketches ", p. 211.

CHAPTER XLIII

Meanwhile things in South Africa were becoming more and more entangled. The Imperial Government was now represented there by Sir Alfred Milner. No man's appointment to an important and difficult post was ever acclaimed with more universal approval. The complimentary " send-off " dinner which was given to him in London on March 27, 1897, was a unique function. Milner and I being old and close friends, who had been contemporaries at Balliol, I was chosen to occupy the Chair. Among the speakers and diners were Mr. Balfour, Mr. Chamberlain, Mr. Morley, Lord Lansdowne and Mr. Goschen. Lord Rosebery and Sir W. Harcourt both sent letters of warm eulogy. " He has the union of intellect with fascination which makes men mount high ": so wrote Lord Rosebery. And Sir W. Harcourt, who never failed in gratitude to those who had served and helped him, as Milner had done in the great Budget of 1894, described him as " a man deserving of all praise and all affection."

During 1898, and the early months of 1899, the grievances of the Outlanders in the Transvaal remained wholly unredressed. They were taxed without representation; they had no voice in the making or working of the laws; their position was described by Sir A. Milner in a famous dispatch as that of " Helots." Constant representations on their behalf were made by Mr. Chamberlain's instructions to President Kruger, but unavailingly, and a conference which was held in May, 1899, between the President and Milner at Bloemfontein, in the hope of arriving at a friendly arrangement, broke down without immediate result. But when Parliament adjourned for the usual autumn recess, no one on either side of politics believed that we were on the brink of war. The sympathies, which would otherwise have gone out so freely to the Outlanders from British Liberals, were chilled by memories of the raid, and suspicions of cosmopolitan finance.

Kruger at last introduced a Franchise Bill into the Volksraad, with a nine years' (afterwards reduced to seven) term of qualification, which Mr. Chamberlain acknowledged to be a possible basis of settlement. Mr. Chamberlain himself firmly believed that the Boers would (if the worst came to the worst) yield to a show of force, and that there would be no real fighting, although it was known that during the last two years they had been making large importations of rifles and other munitions.[1] Even as late as Sep-

---

[1] In a friendly interview at the House of Commons on June 20 between Mr. Chamberlain and " C.-B." (the exact details of which formed the subject of controversy between them five years later [February, 1904]), the word " bluff " was apparently used by " C.-B." and taken up by Chamberlain, who said that the contemplated dispatch of a force to South Africa would be " a game of bluff." (*See* " Campbell-Bannerman ", I, 233-236.)

tember 2, speaking to my constituents, I said: " I for one am not alarmed by the irresponsible clamours which we hear from some familiar quarters for war. I cannot believe that anything has occurred, or is threatened, to bring us even within a measurable distance of a catastrophe, which would be a reproach to statesmanship, a calamity to civilization, and an almost immeasurable catastrophe to South Africa."

Sir W. Harcourt shortly afterwards in a public speech declared that each side had taken up a position in the negotiations which it could not maintain, but that there was no *casus belli*.

But forces had been let loose, largely through faults of language [2] and temper both on the one side and the other, which rapidly escaped control. In substance the proposals urged in September upon the acceptance of the Boer President were reasonable in themselves, and in no way incompatible with the maintenance of the independence of the Transvaal. Ninety-nine people out of a hundred were hoping for, and counting on, a pacific compromise, when, on October 9, Kruger issued an ultimatum which was immediately followed by the Transvaal forces, in combination with those of the Orange Free State, invading British territory.

The Liberal leaders were united and emphatic on one point; in criticizing and condemning Mr. Chamberlain's diplomacy.[3] They were equally unanimous

[2] Mr. Chamberlain's speech at Highbury on August 26, with its provocative metaphors, was a notable example.

[3] Diplomacy which Mr. Chamberlain always stoutly defended. Speaking of his dispatches and speeches, I myself was once rash enough

in denouncing the unpreparedness of the country for war, which the earlier phases of the campaign so disastrously revealed. But their agreement began and ended there, and, as the war went on, their differences became more acute and pronounced. Sir H. Campbell-Bannerman did his best to keep an even middle course. Nor did he ever deviate from the view, which he expressed in his first speech after the reopening of Parliament, that the " Boers had committed an aggression which it was the plain duty of us all to resist." In his own language, used months afterwards to Mr. Herbert Gladstone: " I have been anti-Joe but never pro-Kruger." But in the later phases, he inclined more and more to what was — very unfairly — called the " pro-Boer " attitude, though he maintained throughout friendly and even confidential relations with Lord Rosebery. When the party situation was at its worst, I remember Mr. Morley (with whom I was supposed by the gossips not to be on speaking terms) saying to me one day when we were washing our hands at the Athenæum Club: " Remember that, in this matter, I am not, and never have been, a follower of C.-B." I need hardly say that the implication was that C.-B. was not strenuous enough in his hostility to " Liberal Imperialism ", which Mr. Morley himself had defined (in a speech at Forfar in January, 1900) as " Chamberlain wine with a Rosebery label."

---

to ask in the House of Commons, " What would he not give for the chance of re-editing them to-day? " " I would not alter a word," was his defiant reply.

I can never remember an era in which political nicknames and catchwords were in freer and fuller vogue. Many people enjoyed — probably no one more than Lord Rosebery himself — Mr. Morley's description of him (*à propos* of his somewhat fitful entries and exits) as a " dark horse in a loose box." An old phrase, " Little Englander ", invented, I believe, years before by Mr. Stead during his vivacious editorship of the *Pall Mall Gazette,* was revived, and became a favourite missile in the armoury of Mr. Chamberlain and his bodyguard. He was challenged to define it by Mr. Morley, who said of himself: " I am not a Little Englander; I am an Old Englander, and Old England knew very well what she was about." Mr. Chamberlain, taking up the challenge, described a Little Englander as a man who " honestly believes that the expansion of the Empire carries with it obligations which are out of proportion to its advantages." I joined in this wordy fray, questioning in turn Mr. Chamberlain's title to be a true " Imperialist ", whom I defined as " a man who believes in such expansion only as carries with it advantages not out of proportion to its obligations." [4]

A more adequate appreciation of the magnitude of the task, and of its requirements in men, munitions, and equipment, and the appointment to the control of the operations of Lord Roberts and Lord Kitchener, led in the course of a few months to a

[4] Lord Morley (in after years) in his " Recollections " remarks, with subacid kindliness, that this definition was given " by Mr. Asquith with less than his usual substance and precision." Vol. II, p. 80.

welcome revolution in the military situation. In the speech from the Throne at the close of the session in August, 1900, the Queen was able to say: " My armies have driven back the invaders beyond the frontier they had crossed, and have occupied the two capitals of the enemy and much of his territory." Early in September the annexation of the Transvaal was proclaimed; the war (prematurely, as it turned out) was declared to be over; and Lord Roberts was able to return to take up the functions of Commander-in-chief at home.

The Government resolved on an immediate general election — known in history as the " Khaki Election " of 1900. Liberals of all sections resented advantage being taken of such a moment to elect a new House of Commons. The Duke of Devonshire, the most generally respected member of the Government, gave the official answer with naked *naïveté:* " We all know very well," he said, " that the captain of a cricketing eleven, when he wins the toss, puts his own side in, or his adversaries, as he thinks most favourable to his prospects of winning; and if there is not supposed to be anything unfair about that, then I think the English people would think it very odd indeed if the Prime Minister and leader of a great political party were not to put an electoral question to the country at a moment which he thinks will be not unfavourable to his own side." [5]

The election was held, under strange conditions, and so far as its promoters were concerned, with a

[5] " Life of Devonshire ", II, 278.

somewhat disappointing result. As I have written elsewhere: [6] " There was no cross-fighting between Liberals; and Mr. Chamberlain's invectives, and the famous slogan, ' Every vote given to a Liberal is a vote given to the Boers,' were impartially directed against Liberal candidates of every complexion and shade." On balance, the Opposition as a whole lost no more than four seats.

The actual numbers were:

Ministerialists.		*Anti-Ministerialists.*	
Conservative	334	Liberal and Labour	186
Lib. Unionists	68	Nationalist	82
	402		268

The most notable newcomers in the House of Commons were Mr. Bonar Law and Mr. Winston Churchill.

[6] " Studies and Sketches ", p. 204.